1976

FOURTEEN DAYS

The GREAT THINKERS Series

Alfred north Whitehead

ALFRED NORTH WHITEHEAD

A Primer of his Philosophy

Nathaniel Lawrence
Williams College

◄═○═►

SERIES EDITORS

Arthur W. Brown, Ph.D.
Professor of English and Dean
of the School of Liberal Arts
and Sciences, Baruch College; and
Thomas S. Knight, Ph.D.
Professor and Chairman of the
Department of Philosophy, Adelphi University

Twayne Publishers, Inc.   ::   New York

ISBN-0-8057-3734-0

MANUFACTURED IN THE UNITED STATES OF AMERICA

Foreword

The philosophy of Alfred North Whitehead has had a number of commentators. In the last fifteen years there has been renewed interest and wider recognition. There will be still more. But we must wait until the present social ferment has been quieted before we can consider the general vision which is the hallmark of the truly great philosopher.

Whitehead himself would have been the first to see in the present malaise the prospect of new dreams, new vigor, and new hopes, even in the dismay caused by the melting of old and trusted traditions. That novelty is always necessary and sometimes destructive is an essential part of his philosophy. That evil is as positive as good, but self-destructive by nature, is equally so. He would not have been insensitive to the tragic elements, but they would not have crushed his hope. For this reason he is perhaps even better reading now than he has been in happier times.

It is not Whitehead's modernity that this book has been written to promote, however. Good as the list of commentators is, there seemed to be a clear need for an introduction to Whitehead's philosophy of a sort different from others. An introduction should begin with the elementary and then (as the word implies) lead into more difficult and complex penetrations. The present essay undertakes a slow takeoff and a fairly rapid rate of climb.

The first three chapters of this study include a biography, a general statement of the principal aspects of Whitehead's philosophy (ignoring his highly important work in mathematics and logic), and a presentation of how these principles are embodied in the coming into existence of an "actual occasion"; the remainder of the book is a return to the principal topics of *Process and Reality* (with the exception of the detailed theory of extension). The final six chapters explore these subjects with a double aim in mind: (1) to provide some depth of detail and (2) to show where Whitehead's doctrine seems unclear or assailable. The spirit of these few queries and enquiries is the spirit of enquiry itself, as stated so beautifully in *The Principle of Relativity:* "The worst homage we can pay to genius is to accept uncritically formulations of truths which we owe to it." I hope, in short, to begin a sort of imagined dialogue with the reader which will open his curiosity about Whitehead's philosophy, rather than scholastically satisfying it. In this sense the book aims at the reader's dissatisfaction.

The book, then, leaves off being elementary after Chapter 3, and the pace picks up as we start over the once-covered terrain in greater detail and thoroughness. In this way the reader may be further introduced to philosophy as well as to Whitehead. Throughout, however, I have tried to interpose technical discussion with recognizable illustrations. If such illustrations cannot, on principle, be given, then one may question if it is philosophy.

A second feature, more present perhaps in this book than in others, is an advocacy which is not discipleship. Some of my most marked doubts about Whitehead's philosophy have been allowed to enter, especially where they may have occurred to the reader. Sometimes this advocacy has ventured on the tricky ground of applying Whitehead's thought to areas or in ways that are at best extensions of what he actually did himself. At other times I have had him joining hands with moderns of whom he knew little or nothing. However, there are astonishing parallels between Whitehead and the phenomenologists, for example. My own copies of the works of Sartre, Merleau-Ponty, and others are dotted with hundreds of notations of remarkable parallels. Yet Whitehead's work was independent, vital, original; so I have minimized references to younger philosophers.

Finally, the work has been a personal satisfaction. My previous study of Whitehead's works before *Process and Reality* was an introduction in terms of a fundamental problem that grows in his thought as the thought grows: the relation between mind and body. The present study, focusing primarily on *Process and Reality,* allows me to complete, though not in the technical detail of the earlier work, the examination of that problem. Further, it affords an opportunity to mitigate the unbending scheme of the first book and place Whitehead's philosophy in a position of more open dialogue than before.

The list of Whitehead's works given, with abbreviations for convenience, includes everything referred to in the present study. The complete Whitehead bibliography, edited, with an introduction by Victor Lowe, appears in the second edition of the *Library of Living Philosophers* volume devoted to Whitehead (edited by P. A. Schilpp, New York: Tudor, 1951). I have appended a list of those commentators whose studies have been most helpful to me. The authors include friends, acquaintances, and a former student. I have learned from them all and ask their indulgence where I have differed from them.

As this book was being written, two persons have repeatedly come to my mind. One has finished his life, rich with its personal power, quiet humaneness, and penetrating humor. I am indebted to him in ways too complex to recount. He is part of what Whitehead calls the settled past, with its open-ended, continuing immortality. The other stands at the threshold of maturity in a troubled time. Before her there stretches more uncertainty than I can remember. But this means that there is more that one can leave his own stamp upon. It is a world no longer ready-made. There is in the offing a genuine freedom, which is to say not a world of safety and ease, but of risk and hope. This book is dedicated to this unlikely pair: Clarence Irving Lewis and Mary Ellen Lawrence.

Urschendorf, N.Ö., Austria
and Williamstown, Massachusetts

Acknowledgments

Grateful acknowledgment is made to the following publishers for permission to quote copyrighted materials:

The Macmillan Company for excerpts from:
Adventures of Ideas by Alfred North Whitehead (copyright 1933, by the Macmillan Company).
The Aims of Education and Other Essays by Alfred North Whitehead (copyright 1929, by the Macmillan Company, renewed 1957, by Evelyn Whitehead).
Modes of Thought by Alfred North Whitehead (copyright 1938, by the Macmillan Company).
Process and Reality by Alfred North Whitehead (copyright 1929, by the Macmillan Company).
Religion in the Making by Alfred North Whitehead (copyright 1926, by the Macmillan Company).
Science and the Modern World by Alfred North Whitehead (copyright 1925, by the Macmillan Company).
Symbolism, Its Meaning and Effect by Alfred North Whitehead (copyright 1927, by the Macmillan Company).

Philosophical Library, Inc., for excerpts from:
Essays in Science and Philosophy by Alfred North Whitehead (copyright 1947, by Philosophical Library, Inc.).

Princeton University Press for excerpts from:
The Function of Reason by Alfred North Whitehead (copyright 1929, © 1957, by Princeton University Press).

Thanks are due to the Williams College 1900 Fund for grants which aided in the preparation of the manuscript.

Contents

CHAPTER 1

Biography

Alfred North Whitehead was born on February 15, 1861, at Ramsgate, in the Isle of Thanet, Kent, the son of an Anglican clergyman and schoolmaster.[1] The time and place afforded multiple perspectives. London was 75 miles away, but for much of the life of Kent the distance could have been 750 miles. A cultivated family in this rural setting could provide for its sons the best of two worlds: the civilized riches of the great urban center and the solidarity and common sense of country life.

As to place, the very name "Isle of Thanet" testifies to the provincial sense of history. The "isle" had not been one since the sixteenth century, when the shallow channel between it and the mainland had dried up. As also in the United States, where there are "ports" on the dried-up meanders of the Mississippi, the name has stuck. Moreover, like much of rural England, the local terrain was filled with three-dimensional history. For the people of this world the Norman came late. The fine Norman church at Minster has a Saxon tower, and, as Whitehead remarks, some of its masonry is Roman. Whitehead lived the first fourteen years of his life almost in the shadow of this church, built where Augustine had converted the Saxon King Ethelbert to Christianity. Until early in the nineteenth century, the oak under which this conversion was supposed to have taken place still lived. "All the sermons," says Whitehead in a memoir that dwells on the solidarity of the present with the past, "to be delivered in New England next Sunday morning are derived from that ancestor which still haunts the seawinds in the churchyard of Minster in Thanet." This sense of continuity with the past never deserts Whitehead, and it becomes a cardinal feature of his philosophical doctrine.

The land had absorbed the Roman, the Saxon, the Norman. The space occupied by such land is really captured and congealed time. Not far away lay Canterbury, where Becket was murdered and Edward the Black Prince buried. It was good that the young man was raised with such a sense of historical continuity and of solid history, for he was born at the very edge of a period of intellectual and political change so swift that it would soon antiquate much that had been taken for granted, and institute much that was then hardly even thinkable, let alone predictable.

As a mature philosopher Whitehead would especially dwell on the actuality of time, which includes both the novelty of the present and the unalterable finality of the past. The sense of this actuality begins as far back as his earliest memory. The year is 1864. Whitehead is three years old. His family is returning from Switzerland. The place is Paris. The image he recalls is of soldiers marching along a road from a palace and off into the distance, on a brilliant day of fair trees, sunlight and play. Not recalling that the scene was Paris, the Tuileries, the boy searched many times for this scene, and finally found it, sixteen years later, again on a return from Switzerland, but with the palace and the France of Napoleon III in ruins. Whitehead says he "had caught a glimpse of the pageant of history, and again the second vision gave the tragic interpretation." Here in the concrete feature of his boyhood experience Whitehead learned that historical passage is a mélange of preservation, destruction, transformation, resurrection, and real origination, and that civilization proceeds through the grand economy of these forces. Near the end of his Gifford Lectures, Whitehead summarizes this conflict of delight and brutal loss: "Philosophy may not neglect the multifariousness of the world—the fairies dance, and Christ is nailed to the cross" (PR, 513). The first theme of these lectures is a closely related one, that immortality has death as a prerequisite: "the ever-present, unfading importance of our immediate actions, which perish and yet live for evermore" (PR, 533).

Continuity with the more recent past lay in the sixteenth- and seventeenth-century cottages of Whitehead's boyhood. These were evidently indistinguishable from those of nearby Flanders, and Whitehead says of Sandwich that architecturally it is an old Dutch town. For the men of East Kent the interlocked complexities of London life must have seemed more alien than the independence of the low country towns. Overriding everything else was the sense of one's difference, as a Kent man. The difference was reflected in the concepts of freedom and tolerance which Whitehead recalls from his boyhood. As one reads Whitehead's vignettes of memories, he realizes that although time and place provide the mold which give some early shape to all men, it is the worth of other persons in one's ambience that provides the standards of character.

Real freedom is self-reliance and self-respect rather than mere absence of fetters. The small community in which Whitehead grew up could tolerate the self-willed standards of those whose sense of community was primary. An example, whom Whitehead speaks of touchingly, was "Old Saxby," a man given largely to "beer for plain food and brandy for festive occasions"; "the philosophy of life which he imparted to our ears was that 'eating is a beastly habit.' " Whitehead, himself temperate in all matters, remarks, "You may criticize the moral code of these men when you have risked your life in saving others as often as had that old lifeboats' man." Indeed, strong drink was regarded as a possible aspect of life and not its automatic ruin. During the Napoleonic wars, bootlegging was townwide and was even supported by the clergy. The Minster church services were sometimes interrupted at the approach of revenue officials so that the townspeople might remove the illegal brandy in the church vaults to the peninsular marshes, through which local men alone could find their way. The town was not an outlaw town; but it was seventy-five miles from London, and it did not yield to the pretenses of a central and meddling government. Whitehead tells us that the clerical descendants of these clerical bootleggers were equally filling their role as leaders of the people when, as Whigs, they supported social reform.

Firm self-determination was linked with self-respect. Ecclesiastical differences were strong, abiding, and expected; but they laid the ground for a tolerance of the sort that keeps the peace rather than the indiscriminating tolerance that places equal value on contrasting beliefs. Whitehead tells of an old gentleman named Townsend who vowed never to enter a Nonconformist church and hoped that God would stick him in the doorway (itself a temperate penalty) if he did. And when one of the town's respected Nonconformists died, Mr. Townsend attended the funeral service, but outside the church.

The common bond was of course the land itself. "Geography," says

Whitehead, "is half of character." Elsewhere, he tells of how the Baptist minister at the point of death would see no one but Whitehead's father. The doctrines of Total Immersion and those of baptism in the Established Church could hardly have been further apart. But it was Whitehead's father who came and read the Bible to his dying colleague. "They were," says Whitehead, "both East Kent men; and when they read the Bible together, they understood each other without many words." Notes of this sort, struck in the consciousness of such a sensibility as Whitehead's, resonate throughout a life. In the preface to the Gifford Lectures, fifty years after this death scene, Whitehead echoes the contrast between the firmness of belief deeply reflected upon and the weakness of the mere words that express it: "There remains the final reflection, how shallow, puny, and imperfect are efforts to sound the depths in the nature of things. In philosophical discussion, the merest hint of dogmatic certainty as to finality of statement is an exhibition of folly" (PR, x). Tolerance about beliefs, however firmly held, opens the way for change, growth, and development. Whitehead was in his sixties before he published the great, culminating works of his life. These works end the preoccupation with philosophy of science. They are his statement of a broad cosmology. Much of this work is the evidence of a serious revision as to what is worth writing about. Moreover, when the topics of the earlier and later work overlap, there is doctrinal reversal that verges on contradiction. The late works exhibit an evolution within themselves which is more than a mere unfolding. Late maturity and richness of mind of this sort are partly the fruit of early training in tolerance, the sense of inadequacy of all doctrine to express what it sees.[2]

We get a fine picture, in Whitehead's few published memoirs, of a provincial life that fostered the sense of self-respect, invested not in social level or professional position but rather in the style of one's living. This lost art of style is what prevents political and social subordination from erasing dignity—or making it impossible. England has long been self-aware in this matter; her literature is filled with Jeeveses and Crichtons more admirable than their masters. The same theme is in Whitehead's tale of the old "bobbin" (faggot) man who cut kindling for coal fires, who remarked, "There are some as goes rootling and tearing about. But Lor' bless you, sir, I gets to Saturday night as soon as any of 'em."[3] The old bobbin man's sense of lifestyle is the obvious feature of this story. A little deeper is the image of the objective flow of temporal reality. This reality brooks no man's meddling; it merely provides the dynamic within which a man or a town or a nation designs its style and lives out its time. Whitehead tells the tale as a period piece, a bit of Victoriana.

When we turn from the townspeople to Whitehead's immediate family, we find that the great influences are his father and—more remotely—his grandfather. There is only one reference to his brothers, none to his mother or any female relatives. His grandfather Thomas, whom he regarded as "by far" more remarkable than his father, became headmaster of a private school in Ramsgate at the age of twenty-one. Thomas's son Alfred, who was Whitehead's father, also was appointed headmaster of the same school, at age twenty-five, but later he became an Anglican clergyman. His father and his father's contemporaries, seen in a backward glance, seem to Whitehead to represent vanished types. His father, he says, "was the last example of these East Kent clergymen who were really homogeneous with their people, and therefore natural leaders on all occasions, secular and religious." They knew the lives of their parishioners intimately, lived with them and for them, "saw to it that every child in the village went to school and had an education according to the lights of the day." They constituted, says Whitehead, "a humanizing kindly influence, which trusted mainly to the mercy of God to save the souls of men."

These influences, embodied in the lives of admirable persons, inculcated in the young Whitehead an early awareness of the intimacy of the religious and the educational aspects of life. Such influences underlie a man's choice of profession without necessarily influencing it. Whitehead's first publishing was largely concentrated in logic, mathematics, and the philosophy of science. The interesting exceptions are addresses on the subject of education. At the end of one of these he says:

The essence of education is that it be religious.
   Pray, what is religious education?
   A religious education is an education which inculcates duty and reverence. Duty arises from our potential control over the course of events. Where attainable knowledge could have changed the issue,

ignorance has the guilt of vice. And the foundation of reverence is this perception, that the present holds within itself the complete sum of existence, backwards and forwards, that whole amplitude of time, which is eternity. (AE, 23)

Here the theme of the independence and alterability of the passage of events is closely linked with education, the religious attitude, and freedom. Those hard-nosed philosophers who much later so enthusiastically praised Whitehead's work in the philosophy of science, only to drop away when *Science and the Modern World* with its doctrine of deity appeared, must either never have read this passage, or else have written it off as a rhetorical flourish.

When he was fourteen Whitehead was sent away to school. This was the familiar invitation to the p; th toward maturity. *Going away* to school was as important as going away *to school.* Here, in disciplined surroundings, began the trek toward independence. Now his formal education became a serious and exciting business. This education looks to the world of other places and other times. There is much emphasis on history and the classics, but the interest lies in what can be learned of significance to a young English gentleman on the threshold of English life.

Before Sherburne, Whitehead had already studied Latin for four years, Greek for two. At the Sherburne School, in Dorsetshire, two hundred miles west of Kent, Whitehead thus received his last formal education before his deep plunge into mathematics at Cambridge.

Sherburne had been founded in the seventh century by St. Aldhelm. Alfred the Great was claimed as a former pupil. The bells in the nearby abbey had been brought from Tournai by Henry VIII, returning from the Field of the Cloth of Gold, and the sense of the continuity of the present with the past was given its ultimate undergirding by the very geology of the neighborhood: "more fossils than stones."

In these rich historical environs, "what had not been said in Greek on political philosophy had not been said at all. The Greeks reigned supreme in our minds." Years later Whitehead was to write that the history of philosophy is "a series of footnotes to Plato" (PR, 63). "Athens," says Whitehead, "was the ideal city." Imperial Rome begins with Caesar's murder, which was the end of freedom; *ergo* the boys of Sherburne read Roman history before that time. They understood that

Cicero was "the Roman substitute for a Lord Chancellor." The New Testament was read in Greek. The students also studied mathematics, science, French, and English literature. Only mathematics was well taught. Early on, the classics and mathematics thus became the dominant influences in Whitehead's intellectual development. The physical education and the discipline (including caning) at Sherburne was active and largely in the hands of the students. The students played "football," cricket, and handball. Whitehead became captain of the football and cricket teams, as well as the student "head of the school." Later, at Harvard in his seventies, Whitehead said in a burst of anti-intellectualism: "being tackled at Rugby, there is the Real. Nobody who hasn't been knocked down has the slightest notion of what the Real is . . . I used to play in the middle of the scrum."[4] Those remarks are well worth following a bit further, for they show him explicitly formulating the lessons of his youth, namely that a man is known through his style, and that freedom is shown in identifying yourself with your style. As he says, "They used to hack at your shins to make you surrender the ball, a compulsory element—but the question was how you took it—your own self-creation. Freedom lies in summoning up a mentality which transforms the situation, as against letting organic reactions take their course."[5]

These are, of course, the reflections of an old man, transforming the implicit memories of his childhood into the explicit categories of a mature wisdom. But it is significant how readily Whitehead finds episodes, times, places, and the lessons thereof for the magical concepts of freedom, self-creation, history alive, and the style of living.

Whitehead's talents led to an unusual honor. After five years in Sherburne, he was offered a scholarship to Trinity College, Cambridge, in either classics or mathematics. The subject did not matter—they wanted the man. His father had definite ideas on the subject. Mrs. Whitehead relates her father-in-law's reaction. "Classics, classics! Mathematics, now there's a discipline!" Whether his father's opinion was decisive is not known. Certainly the young man had both unusual talent in, and a real affection for, mathematics.

There followed five years of academic concentration at Cambridge, with an intensity neither known nor permitted in an American university, on mathematics, pure and applied. He says firmly, "I never went inside another classroom." But the concentration is misleading. The rich intellectual life of the college was lived more outside the classroom than in it. Like the sports of Sherburne, the intellectual life of Trinity College was not a matter of regimen or schedule but of interest and self-propelling participation. Dinner each night initiated discussion of a wide-ranging sort among faculty and students. Whitehead speaks of the stimulation of men like D'Arcy Thompson, W. R. Sorley, and Lowes Dickinson. The first two probed deeply into the mathematical and philosophical aspects respectively, of biology. When Whitehead came to Cambridge, the published statement of the theory of evolution was less than two decades old. The excitement of controversy and insight which that theory created are probably impossible to imagine, but when in his philosophical maturity Whitehead developed what he called the "philosophy of organism," he was redacting and reforming the ideas which must have stirred his young mathematician's mind. Thompson's great work, *Growth and Form,* stands today unequaled and unrivaled. It is the fruit of a rare combination of mathematical imagination and biological sensitivity. We can only guess how profoundly the insights of one trenchant, cross-disciplinary mind moved Cambridge students to understand that a single discipline could never satisfy the search for truth.

On Saturday nights a discussion group called the "Apostles" met. The topics varied over a wide range of subjects. The strict membership was limited to twelve undergraduates. But undergraduates and graduates, faculty, distinguished men of affairs, many of them alumni, all came. Henry Jackson and Henry Sidgwick were frequent visitors, and members of Parliament, scientists, and the like, who returned to Cambridge for a weekend of refreshment from their normal lives, thereby provided refreshment for others.

At the end of his five-year term at Cambridge, Whitehead was given a teaching fellowship at Trinity College. The time was 1885. Whitehead was twenty-four years old. His quarter of a century had been one of the highest challenge to the scientific imagination. The Darwinian revolution began two years before his birth. When Whitehead was five, Hoöel translated the work of the geometers Lobachevski and Bolyai into French. As a result, for the first time there was a widespread understanding that geometry as a purely formal discipline did not have to be Euclidean. A year later the independent work of Riemann in the field of non-Euclidean geometry was posthumously published. Seven years before Whitehead was born, George Boole had published his definitive work on the formalization of logic. Leibnitz had dreamed of a universal mathematics. The young Whitehead's own first book-length work was to be entitled *Universal Algebra,* a step toward the realization of this dream.

Clearly the times gave unusual opportunity to the talents of this multi-talented young man, for it was not only mathematics that was in a state of eruption. During Whitehead's first year at Trinity, Michelson and Morley undertook to discover the rate of speed of the earth through the "ether." Their experiment obtained a result which made no sense. It was repeated six years later with essentially the same result. Ultimately, the old concept of a standing "ether," conceived as the medium of transmission for light waves, had to be abolished. The Michelson-Morley experiment resulted in paradoxes which ultimately led to Einstein's presentation of the restricted theory of relativity. This challenge too had to be taken up by any mathematician who was not a mere formalist.

For twenty-five years Whitehead remained at Trinity College. After the first five, in 1890, he married Evelyn Willoughby Wade. Four children were born, all of them at Cambridge: North (December 31, 1891); a second son, unnamed, who died at birth; Jessie (1893); and Eric Alfred (November 27, 1898). Eric became a fighter pilot in World War I and was shot down in March, 1918, over the Forêt de Gobain. Whitehead dedicated his first book in the philosophy of science, *An Enquiry Concerning the Principles of Natural Knowledge,* to the memory of this son.

In 1910 Whitehead was nearly fifty years old. He had written several tracts in geometry and other branches of mathematics, on the order of perhaps sixty to seventy pages in all. He had published one book, *Universal Algebra,* in 1898. His entire career as philosopher and humanist lay before him virtually unopened. As this point he made a decisive move. He left Cambridge and went to London. The first volume of *Principia Mathematica,* written with Russell, appeared in this critical year. The following year, 1911, would see the publication of his elementary and highly readable *Introduction to Mathematics;* 1912 would bring the second volume of *Principia Mathematica;* 1913, the third. His articles for the *Encyclopaedia Britannica,* "The Axioms of Geometry," "Mathematics," and "Non-Euclidean Geometry" (with Russell), were written in this same culminative surge.

But now two questions arose which provoked Whitehead's interest beyond mere formal thought. Since the Euclidean system of geometry is but one logically coherent system among many possible ones, which geometry (or more generally, which axiomatic system) is demanded by the actual facts of nature? In short, which abstract system fits? Obviously, this question can not itself receive a purely formal answer, and its relevance had been intensified by the publication of Einstein's paper of 1905 on the "special" theory of relativity. The second question was one of practical pedagogy: how can mathematics be made more understandable, less forbidding? It is from a concern with the teaching of mathematics that Whitehead's interest in education as a whole stems. In 1911 the *Introduction to Mathematics* presented in a clear and simple way the main features of what was already known in mathematics. No research was involved. The task was one of pedagogy. As Whitehead says in the opening sentence of the book, "The study of mathematics is apt to commence in disappointment." And later, "The reason for this failure of the science to live up to its reputation is that its fundamental ideas are not explained to the student disentangled from the technical procedure which has been invented to facilitate their exact presentation in particular instances." Persistent inquiry into problems of teaching ultimately leads to questions of how we think, and this in turn leads to questions of human nature.

For Whitehead, mathematics was thus the beginning and the broad base of a career, not its end. His interests after 1913 lead in two directions: to nature and to human nature. Formal geometries are equally logically valid. Which is true, to what extent, and because of what facts in the world? The answers must ultimately lie in "nature perceived," not just in nature thought about. As Whitehead says in the *Introduction to Mathematics,* "the 'spaciness' of space does not enter into our geometrical *reasoning* at all" (242). Persons learn, are educationally nourished, and are developed, ill or well. How does this happen? Why? How can it be improved?

These two growing interests, nature and human nature, follow different channels for a considerable period. In 1912 Whitehead gave two addresses, later published, on mathematics in relation to education generally. Later there appeared in the *Mathematical Gazette* his presidential address of 1916 to the Mathematical Association, "The Aims of Education," which ranges over the whole of education. More essays in education follow, but always at a level of popular expression and for popular audiences.

Whitehead's interest in nature, however, follows a more technical line. It is concerned with the meaning of relativity, on the one hand, and with the relation between nature encountered and nature systematized, on the other.

The bulk of Whitehead's work on the problems and theory of education, and the philosophy of science, fall into a period of a dozen years, from 1910 to 1922. During the first year of this period he did not teach. We may assume that the giant labor of his share in volumes II and III of *Principia Mathematica* was occupying much of his energy. In 1911 he returned to teaching, at University College, London. In 1914 he became a professor at the Imperial College of Science and Technology in Kensington, a position he held until he came to the United States. He also held several advisory and administrative posts in other colleges at the same time.

A third major feature of Whitehead's development up to this point has hardly appeared at all, in either address or publication. This feature is Whitehead's concern with religion. According to Mrs. Whitehead, she and her husband read widely and intensively in the literature of Catholicism for a period of seven years, from 1891 to 1898. Both of them were somewhat disaffected with Anglicanism. The interest in Catholicism was not, therefore, merely scholarly or cultural, but was undertaken with a view to possible formal espousal of the Roman faith. The conversion did not occur; nonetheless, it was in this period that the first ideas were born which were to emerge with little external warning nearly thirty years later in *Religion in the Making*. The reading of this period naturally radiated outward into cultural history, and it seems likely that here Whitehead gained the exceptional comprehension of history which so frequently astonished even his closest friends.[6] Many of the dominant ideas of *Adventures of Ideas* (1933) were, Mrs. Whitehead says, shaped in this early period. Whitehead, in his essays on

education, likes to deal with the educative process as the outcome of a
natural "ferment." The term is evidently partly autobiographical. And
when Whitehead says, with almost unparalleled opacity, in the preface
to *Adventures of Ideas,* that Paul Sarpi's *History of the Council of
Trent* was one of the half-dozen books that most influenced his
"general way of thinking," it is to the last decade of the nineteenth
century that we must turn for the origins of this interest and this
influence.

The last period of Whitehead's life begins in 1924, when he was
sixty-three years old. Up to this point he stands, with Russell, as the
founding father in the new logic, as a practical educator of experience
and responsibility, as well as a polished and provocative analyst of the
educational process. He has, in addition, a reputation as a philosopher
of science. Thus far his stature is great, but his mind has reached few
men and his direct influence is small. Since he is a civil servant,
mandatory retirement faces him in two years. At this point an
invitation to join the Harvard faculty arrives.

As early as 1920 James K. Woods, then chairman of the Department
of Philosophy at Harvard University, had written to President Lowell to
explore the possibility of bringing Whitehead to Harvard.[7] But the
financial aspects of the problem could not be solved. Three years later
those friends of Josiah Royce who had constituted themselves after his
death as the Royce Club, renewed the effort. Lawrence Henderson and
two other members of the club, together with Henry Osborn Taylor, set
the wheels in motion again, this time successfully.[8] Whitehead had
visited the United States in the interim, in 1922, and had given a lecture
at Bryn Mawr. He was very favorably impressed: he "fell in love with
America," according to his son. His acceptance of an invitation,
accordingly, seemed probable. Furthermore, the financial difficulty was
solved by Professor Taylor's undertaking to pay at least a substantial
part of Whitehead's salary.[9]

The offer from Harvard was for a five-year appointment. Whitehead
came, in the spirit of adventure, and to satisfy a long-standing desire to
teach philosophy. A short time before the official offer he had written
a friend at Harvard, Mark Barr, that he felt disinclined to teach students
the thoughts of other men but that he would welcome the
"opportunity of developing in systematic form my ideas on Logic, the

Philosophy of Science, Metaphysics, and some more general questions, half philosophical and half practical, such as Education. . . ." It is an index of the fecundity and creativity of his mind that Whitehead's program of interests was only lopsidedly fulfilled, in spite of his longevity. Strictly formal logic, in the years to come, played virtually no part in his thinking, although Whitehead the philosopher of logic and exploiter of logical form shows through in *Process and Reality,* in the eccentric theory of propositions and in the "Method of Extensive Connection." But in this final period Whitehead's philosophy of science becomes a department of metaphysics and not an autonomous discipline. *Science and the Modern World* and *Adventures of Ideas* would indeed probe "more general questions," but alas, all too little in the vital area of education. Undoubtedly these projects had to be treated lightly to make way for the new interest in his final phase: religion. This preoccupation had apparently not been anticipated by Whitehead, at least as a subject for publication. Not only does the final period see the publication of *Religion in the Making,* but religion plays a critical role in three other books, including *Process and Reality.*

At Harvard, Whitehead's work attained an early and lasting success. After two years of teaching he was asked to stay as long as he was able. Instead of five years, Whitehead taught for thirteen, completing in this period, between his sixty-third and his seventy-sixth years, all of his work in philosophy proper, in several articles and tracts, and in seven books: *Science and the Modern World; Religion in the Making; Symbolism, Its Meaning and Effect; The Function of Reason; Process and Reality; Adventures of Ideas;* and *Modes of Thought.* Almost all of this material appeared first in the form of invitational lectures in colleges and universities on both sides of the Atlantic.

In his teaching at Harvard Whitehead habitually left his best students reaching for the fullness of his meaning; he frequently overestimated their training or their readiness, but he never failed to stimulate even the least able of his listeners in some measure. He evidently spoke as one having authority. But his manner was one of candor, modesty, and freshness. Whitehead says, in one of his essays on education, that the ideal of a college professor is "an ignorant man, thinking." This quality of using the classroom as a place to think was one of his notorious characteristics and a contagious one. He combined sharp and penetrating criticism with a kindly and sometimes overgenerous discernment of excellence. More than one student found the weak points in his thoughts nearly mercilessly exposed and his work graded A+. There was a touch of the pixie in Whitehead, and it gleams in the legends that have already gathered around him. Perhaps these paradoxical evaluations were his novel way of dealing with the inequities of the grading system.

Together with W. E. Hocking, Whitehead taught joint seminars, perhaps some of the first "team teaching" in the country. Both men found these encounters not only rewarding but the cause of a genuine alteration of view. "The dialogue was real," says Professor Hocking.

After his retirement in 1937, Whitehead lived for another ten years in Cambridge. His home, even through a gradual decline in physical powers, was a meeting place for men of all ages, professions, and degrees of distinction. Visitors came from far and near, always to find themselves refreshed and challenged by the unflagging originality of Whitehead's mind and by the warmth of his personality.

Whitehead died on December 30, 1947. It is unlikely that this century will see another thinker with such an astonishing array of talent to bring to the giant scope of philosophy. It is even less likely that a great thinker will appear with such sustained powers of growth, development, and creativity.

CHAPTER 2

The Philosophy of Organism

I *Speculative Philosophy*

Whitehead's mature philosophy he thought of as a speculative philosophy. "Speculative" has a chancy sound. A stock-market speculator is one who *guesses* what market values will be some time in the future. A speculative answer to a question is one whose grounding is not sound, even if the answer is correct. To speculate is to guess. Perhaps speculative philosophers have given speculation a bad name. In any case, speculative philosophy means something very different from guessing.

In Latin *specula* means, literally, a watchtower, a point of view which is broadly inclusive and one which displays the scene around us in proper perspective. At ground level, on which the *specula* stands, we see only a little. We see it in much detail, to be sure, but the little we see, being close at hand, is disproportionately large in our vision. Sacrificing the detail, we may see things from the watchtower from which they are both more remote and more in true size with respect to one another. Philosophy must be speculative if it is to be general. It must see far and inclusively, but it cannot be merely speculative. Whitehead says, in a homely simile:

The true method of discovery is like the flight of an aeroplane. It starts from the ground of particular observation; it makes a flight in the thin air of imaginative generalization; and it again lands for renewed observation rendered acute by rational interpretation. (*PR*, 7)

Speculative philosophy must necessarily be opposed to the restrictions of some special way of looking at the world, especially those views based on strategic simplifications. For example, it will regard an *exclusively* moral approach to values as monocular, or a *purely* "scientific" view of the world as limiting itself to too small a part of possible experience.

Moreover, it is a mistake to suppose that speculative philosophy is impractical. It concerns itself not only with what is but with what might be, or—in its own language—with the possible as well as the actual. A modern young man who says "It's a lousy world" is holding the actual world as he sees it against a possible (and better) world. If one research team says "We can lick cancer" and another "We can land on Mars," they are making claims about the realm of the possible as related to the actual. It is not merely a matter of courage, hope, determination, and so on. It is also a matter of judgment and vision. Such vision requires at least a modest *specula*. No one is always flat on the ground. He is, to some extent, always speculative. He may be a poor philosopher, or an unadventurous one, who borrows his convictions uncritically. But the need to see things in the large and in a balanced way is common to all men. Creative or imitative, active or passive, we cannot avoid having some general overall view of how things are and how they might be.

Speculative metaphysics is, then, a natural outgrowth of normal human thinking. But in its search for ultimate generality, it is ambitious beyond the level of common sense and even beyond the level of inquiry in the special fields of human thought.

To borrow a term from Whitehead, what speculative metaphysics wants is *generality of outlook*. This is what he means when he says, in *Process and Reality,*

At the end, in so far as the enterprise has been successful, there should be no problem of space-time, or of epistemology, or of causality, left over for discussion. The scheme should have developed all those generic notions adequate for the expression of any possible interconnection of things." (vii)

(1) "Generic notions" means of course principal, basic ideas, landmarks of unusual height, seen from the *specula*. (2) When Whitehead says "in so far as the enterprise . . . ," he is warning us of the scope of what he has undertaken. He is not giving us the pretentious guarantee of success. (3) Finally, "possible interconnection" carries us

back again to the theme already developed. As soon as we find ourselves comparing things as they are with things as they possibly might be, we are on the frontiers of speculative metaphysics. When we refuse to consider things as we find them, from the limited point of view of some special science, we are nearing the heartland of speculative philosophy.

II *The Two Aspects of Whitehead's Thought*

In a speculative philosophy the great problem is to build the lookout tower firmly enough so that it can support one, and high enough so that one can see what there is and imagine, at least roughly, what lies beyond. Whitehead realizes that such surety and comprehensiveness is unattainable. "Philosophers," he says, "can never hope finally to formulate these metaphysical first principles. Weakness of insight and deficiencies of language stand in the way inexorably" (*PR,* 6). We shall see in what follows that Whitehead wishes to correct certain widespread types of "weakness of insight" and that a good deal of his philosophy can be approached through his efforts to improve insight, especially where it comes from lookout towers unhappily built in the bottoms of narrow valleys. "Deficiencies of language" are insuperable also, but this does not mean that we must simply yield to them. "The position of metaphysics," says Whitehead, "in the development of culture cannot be understood without remembering that no verbal statement is the adequate expression of a proposition"; that is, "no language can be anything but elliptical, requiring a leap of the imagination to understand its meaning in its relevance to immediate experience" (*PR,* 20). We shall find, accordingly, that Whitehead employs familiar words in ways more general than we are used to, for the sake of bringing to light and clarifying hidden and only half-felt meanings in familiar words and phrases. For the most part, Whitehead invents new words, but he stretches many, sometimes to cover areas of our experience which we profoundly sense yet have no familiar way of describing and discussing.

The fact that generality of outlook requires a generalized or, in some cases, *re*generalized vocabulary brings us to two important polarities in Whitehead's thought. I shall call these the scientific and the humane, or humanistic.

We have already seen that Whitehead lived the greater part of his professional life as student, scholar, teacher, and creative thinker in mathematics and theoretical physics. His talents were extraordinary, and in some respects they were unique. His contributions are permanent. Over against these accomplishments and the talents which gave rise to them, there were in him also the qualities of mind and person as well as the training and education which go into the making of a great humanist. These human interests were evident from the beginning; they gave shape and substance to a total philosophy, late in a brilliant and creative life. His mature philosophy is a synthesis of these two counterfoiled aspects of human thought, which—like the two legs on which men walk—must be in coordination if progress is to be made.

If we devote ourselves exclusively to either major type of pursuit, we run certain avoidable risks. Whitehead's synthesis of the two is intended to place each in the perspective of the other, so that the reality seen by the one is not assumed to be subordinate or reducible to the other.

(1) In science and in mathematics, the more exact and general we become, the more we seem to deal with things and ideas which can be grasped only by inference, reflection, and sometimes even sheer construction. Nothing in our ordinary experience seems to correspond to them. To begin with, they are quite intangible. Such things as equations, protons, inequalities, and vectors are thin and rare occurrences in our general experience, so densely populated with trees and people, tables and streams. Not only are these abstract entities less tangible, but they are more removed, less immediate than such vital and commonplace intangibles as hope and hatred, choosing and sharing. For this reason, humanistic thinkers are likely to regard the entities of science and of mathematics as unreal, constructed concepts, clever myths that caricature reality without really presenting it. "But if it is something else you mean," says Whitehead, "for heaven's sake say it" (*CN*, 45). Humanistic thinkers who wave away the scientific expositions of the natural world as "merely conceptual" face on insuperable problem: the enormous success of science in the domain of *results*. These results are as tangible as trees and as immediate as pleasure.

(2) The humane approach to philosophy, by contrast, lacks success in prediction. Moreover, it entertains apparent contradictions—for example, that a man may both love and hate his brother, or that an

historical event has both splendid and vicious consequences—and seems to be forever dealing with what is ambiguous, dubious, and unclear. Devotees of the scientistic approach are fond of claiming that meanings in a world so conceived tend to be arbitrarily subjective and naturally vague.

This conflict, which has unhappily been called that of the two cultures, is of course nothing of the kind. It is a conflict, like all genuine conflict, of men—men narrowed by professional persuasion and uneasy and apprehensive about the values on the other side of the wall. The remedy for this conflict is a speculative lookout tower of sufficient scope to render the wall insignificant, except as a monument to professional pride. The perspective gained is needed in order to see beyond generalizations hastily and narrowly drawn up. Only in this way can the genuine truths on either side be appreciated.

Such a task demands the release of key notions from their restricted use in specialized fields. Ideas and concepts having peculiar significance in a limited area of thought must be shown in their larger context. Consider such notions as "life," "temporality," "organism," "physicality," "mentality," "freedom," "creativity," "mechanism," "value," "fact," "novelty," "God."

Every one of these terms has a special meaning as it appears in one discipline or another. The biologist, for example, defines life in terms of the capacity of individuals to replicate by synthesis from their environment. For the religious man life is a gift, a miracle. "Freedom" means one thing for the political philosopher, another for the physicist (who speaks of the "degrees of freedom" of a particle); while the social reformer means still a third thing by "freedom," close to the political meaning, but different from it. If our language is not to fall into the confoundment of Babel, we must get beyond the special dialects of the professions. The task of speculative philosophy is to provide the general framework of understanding within which a *community* of special discipline is possible. "Philosophy," says Whitehead, "is the critic of abstractions."

The rest of this chapter undertakes to give a bold outline of Whitehead's philosophy in terms of some key notions, including those in the above list.

III   *Some Key Notions*

For Whitehead the real world is a world whose reality is time-structured. No conviction is more fundamental and unyielding throughout the entire development of his thought. Reality is through and through temporal. The title of *Process and Reality* could as well have been *Process Is Reality*. There is a realm, as we shall see, of the eternal and also of the everlasting (which ought not to be confused with one another), but they exist primarily in relation to the one open, unending actual world whose essential feature is its real passage.

(1) *Life*. This real world of processive passage is both similar to, and different from, that of the Greeks. The Greek word *bios*, from which we take the words "biology," "antibiotic," and so on, is usually translated into the narrowly English word "life." But its range is much larger. Plato unhesitatingly speaks of the *psyche* ("soul") of what we should ordinarily call "living things." But he also speaks of the *psyche* of the *polis* ("city-state," e.g., Athens) in the *Republic,* and also of a world psyche in the *Timaeus*. The psyche is the livingness of what is otherwise dead or inanimate.[1] For Plato, living man lives within the living social *polis,* and ultimately in the *cosmos,* the world alive. Life is no mere biological category. Whatever *lives* is self-moving, that is, in some sense is self-creating and self-maintaining. This theme is echoed in Aristotle's famous remark that nature *(phusis)* is like a doctor doctoring himself *(Physics* 199b30-32). The whole of nature as alive is the primary case of life, not a metaphor drawn from the more short-lived individual living things.

This view of the world, called *panpsychism,* Whitehead espouses and develops, but in a wholly modern way. Whitehead restores to the word "life" that broader set of meanings through which the Greek saw himself as living within living nature. For both Whitehead and the classical philosophers it then appears that man's acute alienation or separateness from nature is not normal but pathological. It has no natural basis in the relations between man and the world. As Whitehead says, in dealing with types of organization of things in nature, whether they be electrons or persons, "ther is no absolute gap between 'living' and 'non-living' . . ." (*PR,* 156). How *living* any such ordered collection (in Whitehead's vocabulary a "society") may be depends on the degree of novelty which it originates during the time of its existence. In so speaking of "living" and "non-living," Whitehead is paying close attention to a point of considerable importance for modern theoretical biology, which is not usually approached or viewed from a very high *specula.* The point is this: We tend to accept the supposition that life (at least on this planet) was not introduced but emerged gradually from nonliving matter, perhaps by way of a chemical progression from simple amino acids to complex protein molecules. Somewhere in past time these protein molecules, or their forebears, crossed the theshold of life and became self-replicating. The more we hold that this emergence was gradual, the more we accept Whitehead's notion of the blurred boundary between life and nonlife. We are thus brought to the second expanded term which Whitehead wishes to probe for its deeper meanings: temporality.

(2) *Temporality: the shape of time.* The emergence of the living from the nonliving immediately exposes a crucial modernity in Whitehead's thought, distinguishing him from the Greeks. Evolutionary theory as normally conceived, apart from all reference to arguable details, rests on a modern view of time. Classical philosophy really had no notion of abstract empty time (this notion we owe primarily to Sir Isaac Newton); accordingly, we would be wiser to speak of the classical notion of temporality, hoping to designate thereby the concrete passage of events, changing and recurring. "Temporality" has more and richer qualities than those of sheer abstract succession. This is the mode in which we normally experience temporal passage. From such temporal passage we can of course distill or abstract Newtonian and other scientific conceptions of "time," but such distillation requires the raw materials of actual temporal experience to begin with. Viewed this way, temporality seems to move in great cycles. Everything that lives comes into being, grows, develops, matures, declines, and dies. There is an endless cyclicity of life, whether it be the micro-life of an annual plant that fulfills its role in one calendar year, or the macro-life of a *polis,* a city-state, like Plato's Republic, whose cycle may fill many years. Nature is the scene of an eternal return. Nature herself seems to be everlastingly alive, she alone not coming to birth or dying, but all else that lives within her following the cycle of rebirth. Temporal passage seen as circular is rendered even more concrete and immediate in the

rotations of the heavenly bodies by which we measure great units of time (e.g., the notion of a "light-year" rests on that of a "year," which is the time of the earth's [somewhat] circular path around the sun).

We use this circularity of time as a convenient reference for all kinds of measurement of time, whether it be the rotating hands of a clock or rotations on a grand astronomical scale. The circularity of time infiltrates our commonest modes of speech; for example, we say, "Why! the *same* thing happened at the *same* time yesterday!" Nonetheless, we also believe in the uniqueness of each successive moment of time. This conviction adapts better to the metaphor of a straight line, or rather to motion along a straight line, than it does to that of motion in a circle. In rectilinear motion each point is passed once and only once. In circular motion the points represent endlessly repeatable phases of the temporal process.

For the most part, Whitehead does not undertake to solve or adjudicate the competing metaphors of "circle" and "straight line" for temporal passage. There is some indication that, as he developed his thought beyond the philosophy of science, he became more and more aware of the limitations of trying even to represent time spatially, or to derive broad meanings for temporality from the restricted perspective of scientific measurement. It is clear, however—and this is all that we need for the moment—that the unique features of temporality increasingly seemed to him to dominate the recurrent ones. He says, for example, "nature is never complete. It is always passing beyond itself. This is the creative advance of nature. Here we come to the problem of time" (*PR*, 443). The key notion here is the conception of "creativity," to which we shall return in a moment. To take "creativity" seriously is to take the novel occurrences in temporality—those things which never existed before—equally seriously. Plato believed in an immortality of life and in the transmigration and rebirth of psyches which had lived before, but such psyches were stripped of their individuality by an erasure of memory in order to be born anew, afresh (*Republic* X). Individual uniqueness was thus for Plato a secondary and dispensable factor in the eternal return. The primary thing was the cycle, the recurrent. The Christian conception of immortality, on the other hand, holds to the primary and inalienably unique character of each human life. The *time* of such a life is thus a set of unique, never-to-be-repeated moments.

Post-Newtonian, rectilinear time is an interesting offspring of this Christian time composed of unique moments. It keeps the uniqueness of each temporal moment—so that time can be represented either as motion along a line or as a line itself (a "coordinate")—but strips such temporality of all reference to persons or things.

To summarize thus far, Whitehead, like the Greeks, is committed to the idea of temporal processes as being the real basis for any abstract metrical time. But, unlike the Greeks, his notion, to be developed below, that creativity means the production of what is genuinely novel and unique, leads him to deal with temporal processes as rectilinear rather than as circular.

Temporality: the divisibility of time. Another question that must be dealt with in any cosmology is that of temporal divisibility. From the age of Zeno to the present the mathematical presentation of time is of a continuum which can be divided without limit. If we imagine a time-line (circular or rectilinear, it makes no difference), then we can also imagine the "points" of such a line as instantaneous moments "on" or "in" the line. But we ask now: "Is there anything in nature which corresponds to such an instantaneous moment?" Whitehead's answer is "No." There are legitimate ways of deriving and applying such conceptions as those of a dimensionless point in space or an unenduring moment in time. But there is nothing in nature which immediately answers to these complex geometrical notions. Supposing that there is leads to the famous paradoxes of Zeno and to the misconstruction of the true character of our experience.

The world is a fabric of interconnected and interdependent events. Larger events have smaller ones as constituents. The least unit of the real, Whitehead calls an "actual occasion." It is, he says, "the limiting type of an event with only one member" (*PR,* 113). These actual occasions may also be called "actual entities." The two terms are exchangeable, except that the latter term includes God as well.[2] Since they are the *least* units of actuality, actual occasions do not materialize gradually; that is, they cannot come into existence one part after another. Rather, they come "all at once." Whitehead says they "atomize the extensive continuum" (*PR,* 104). This is a misleading statement, since it suggests that the extensive continuum—space-time—was somehow "there" all along, before the events which fill it. But this is not Whitehead's account of the matter. The converse is the case. The *basic* reality is the processive flow of events. The fundamental fact of nature is her passage. The spatiotemporal continuum is itself obtained only through a complex intellectual abstraction from this fundamental passage. It is therefore nearer the truth to say that space and time are "in" events rather than that events are "in" space and time. What William James says about irreducibly minimal units of experience Whitehead says about actual entities in this "epochal theory of time." Whitehead quotes James in order to explicate his own view: "Either your experience is of no content, of no change, or it is a perceptible amount of content or change. Your acquaintance with reality grows literally by buds or drops of perception. Intellectually and on reflection you can divide these into components, but as immediately given, they come totally or not at all." (*PR*, 105-6). The world as Whitehead sees it is thus composed of least units which display spatiotemporal extension analogous to the "buds or drops of perception." The abstract space and time which we extract from the flow of events can of course be divided, without limit, *in thought,* but the actual events from which they are derived cannot. Whitehead puts it succinctly: "the creature is extensive, but . . . its act of becoming is not extensive" (*PR*, 107).

A simple formula results, provided we understand the terms employed. Units of temporality are like our units of experience; they come in minimal but extended chunks. The abstract "time" we derive from temporality is indefinitely divisible. The temporality from which it is derived is not.

(3) *Organism and Mechanism.* It is a striking feature of Whitehead's development as a philosopher that although he comes to philosophy by way of mathematics and physics, his mature philosophy reaches beyond the limited vocabulary of those disciplines when it searches for terms to stretch in the service of cosmology. The unreduced vocabularies of biology and psychology afford richer opportunities for expressing what he wants to exhibit.[3]

If the conviction that there is no sharp line of distinction between "living" and "non-living" is taken seriously, then what kind of term should be expanded as a general term covering all kinds of entities? We have already seen that Whitehead uses the terms "actual occasion" (or "actual entity" where the latter term differs from the former) only in designating God as well. "Occasion" suggests an event, an occurrence. "Entity" has a less dynamic ring to it, and Whitehead exploits both these ways of looking at an actual entity. Both conceptions are needed, namely: the basic unity of reality as having a temporal structure in itself, a dynamic; and also the entity as being completed, closed up, or, to use Whitehead's technical term, "satisfied." Yet one thing is missing, the notion of order. What kind of order, what kind of organization, do these entities display, both within themselves and among themselves? As between two candidates, "mechanical order" and "organic order," the latter term is obviously more attractive to someone who sees the universe as alive. But the choice should not rest upon a mere preference based on an unexamined conviction.

Mechanism. Strictly speaking, a mechanism is a thing made. Its operations are wholly explainable in terms of what has happened to it prior to its operating. Each state of its activity is interpretable, on principle, as the outcome of prior states within the limits of its structure. To the extent that we give a causal analysis of mechanical activity, we look to past conditions that brought forth the present ones and to still further past conditions which generated the more recent ones. If the categories of intention, purpose, aim, or end are employed, they refer to how and why the machine came to be made, the function it was designed to serve. In the distinction to be found as far back as Aristotle, machines operate through efficient causes, "that-by-reason-of-which." Their "final cause," "that-for-the-sake-of-which," they do not have internal to them. Mechanical processes are repetitions exclusively dependent upon antecedent processes. The scientific view of the world concentrates on the idea of efficient cause as being the only fundamental type of cause.

Organism. Organisms are at least superficially different. They may involve and include many subordinate mechanisms, but the total problem of organic order looks to the future as well. We say a seed puts down roots in order to obtain food and water, that the plant later develops leaves "for" food manufacture and storage. This corresponds more closely to Aristotle's "that-for-the-sake-of-which." We generally bury this conception under the term "function." The function of a root is to provide moisture and nourishment; the function of the heart is to circulate the blood through the body; the function of circulation is to . . . and so on. All the same this is *telic* analysis, an analysis in terms of a *telos*, an end-in-view, rather than an analysis purely and simply in terms of "that-on-account-of-which." Once we concentrate on the metaphor of mechanism, we must not only decapitate the metaphor (by ignoring the fact that all machines bear evidence of a design or a purpose external to them), we must further undertake to reduce all cause and all function exclusively to the prior conditions under which they appeared. Any function of an organism as a whole, or in any of its parts, is then treated as only a type of operation which the organism accidentally developed and which provided it with some assistance (or at least noninterference) in surviving—or alternatively provided its species such assistance.

Let us stop here and summarize the defense of the selection of the word "organism" to refer to the fundamental units of reality—the actual entities. The point is simple. As we look at things about us we find we need both the notions of "that-on-account-of-which" and of "that-for-the-sake-of-which." Organisms require both; mechanisms need only the former. "Organism" is already thus the larger term, requiring less stretching. If we take the more restricted term "mechanism," we have to explain away too much that is evidently not merely mechanical in our own experience.

The foregoing presentation has as its aim the illumination of some of the most terse and difficult passages in Whitehead's philosophy. Consider, for example: "In the philosophy of organism it is held that the notion of 'organism' has two meanings, interconnected but intellectually separable, namely, the microscopic meaning and the macroscopic meaning" (*PR*, 196). "According to this account, efficient causation expresses the transition from actual entity to actual entity ['macroscopic meaning'] ; and final causation expresses the internal process whereby the actual entity becomes itself ['microscopic meaning'] " (*PR*, 228). Whitehead's summary statement of this notion introduces several themes not yet discussed. It is included here to show how efficient and final causation are both requisite modes of analysis and how they draw together past and future:

To sum up: There are two species of process, macroscopic process, and microscopic process. The macroscopic process is the transition from attained actuality to actuality in attainment; while the microscopic process is the conversion of conditions which are merely real into determinate actuality. The former process effects the transition from the "actual" to the "merely real"; and the latter process effects the growth from the real to the actual. The former process is efficient; *the latter process is teleological.* The future is merely real, without being actual; whereas the past is a nexus of actualities. (*PR,* 326-27; italics mine)

The above passages are tough and cannot be at present fully explicated, but they give us substance from Whitehead for the following summary: an effort to explain the world exclusively in terms of past occurrences ignores the tendencies toward the future which are present in all present processes. This future-tending character of things is what is traditionally called their teleological causation. Since teleology can be ignored only at the expense of balanced explication, the term "organism" includes all the major implications we need for dealing with what is actually before us in experience. Further, it suggests that an organic universe is alive, thus restoring the classical insight into the relation between man and nature.

But "organism" has two distinguishable (not separated) meanings. The individual actual entites are organisms. Each of them is "at once the product of the efficient past, and is also, in Spinoza's phrase, *causa sui*" (*PR,* 228). As cause of itself, for its own sake, the actual entity introduces teleology into the world. "Organism" also refers to the organic relations between and among actual entities, as well as within them. But of course the novelty appears against a backdrop of predictability, and this predictability is evidence of the thoroughgoing presence of over-arching order among such entities, permeated through and through by efficient causation, the iron hand of the past on the present. Indeed it is only from the backdrop of a stable universe that any creative novelty can arise.

(4) *Physical and Mental.* Thus far we have dealt with actual entities as the basic units of process, organically exhibiting both efficient cause and final or teleological composition in their behavior. We turn now to the meanings—extended meanings—for the notions of "physical" and "mental."

Much of Whitehead's philosophy is directed toward a systematic presentation of the world which will do no violence to the world of common sense. The world of common sense is of course often misconstrued, and people often agree—even for centuries—about this world, and yet are in error. A philosophy which emerged as the mere expression of common sense inherits more puzzles than it solves. What is it that is present in common sense that should be incorrigible—incapable of being reasoned away? The manifest qualitative and quantitative features of experience. The colors, sounds, textures, tastes of things are as real as their shapes and their numbers and their temporal endurance. Whitehead is here, in this respect, a follower of Berkeley. Berkeley had shown that Locke's distinction of the qualities of the experienced world into primary and secondary characteristics—the former being regarded as more "real" than the latter—was a total failure. The whole of our experience stands or falls together, insofar as it is simply given. Some aspects of it may be more fluctuating than others. Some aspects may lend themselves more readily to faulty judgment; for example, shapes seem to be more reliable, by and large, than colors of things. But therefore to sweep these more variable data aside as unreal, or secondary, or illusory, is indefensible, arbitrary.

Even in the period when he confined his attention to philosophy of science, in *The Principles of Natural Knowledge* and in *The Concept of Nature,* Whitehead parted company with those scientistically minded speculators who prefer to invest only scientific objects with primary reality—the rest of the world being supposedly "composed" of such objects and their relations. Any systematic view of the world must be able to include both the world as perceived by common sense and the world as reasoned out by scientific study. Any "bifurcation of nature," as Whitehead calls it in these works, into nature conceived and nature perceived is *prima facie* false. There is but one nature, he says, that "which is before us in perceptual knowledge" (*CN*, 40).[4] These convictions, forged when Whitehead was explicitly not undertaking a metaphysics, but only a philosophy of nature (*CN*, 31-32), never deserted him. The main features of our ordinary experience cannot be reduced to illusion nor regarded as the mere outcome of a causal action of external nature upon the internalities of our mind.

As Whitehead progresses from philosophy of science to metaphysics he generalizes the rejection of a bifurcated world. He shows that if the incipient self-making and telically ordered existence which we associate with living things is not to be found *in micro* in the simple units of reality, we will be wholly unable to explain their presence in the more complex entities which we commonly encounter. Very similar considerations underlie his treatment of the physical and mental aspects of the world. For example, from the time of Descartes to the present, philosophers have trapped themselves into incoherence on the subject of the relation between body and mind. If the mental and physical are utterly distinct, the former thinking and unextended, the latter extended and unthinking, as Descartes says, then how is there a connection between the two? How does my purely mental intent become fulfilled in a physical fact "out there," or the physical body get recorded or presented as a nonphysical idea "in" my mind?

This polar controversy cannot be historically reviewed here. Whitehead's response to the problem is like that of William James in one respect: a steadfast refusal to regard either the mental or the physical as ultimate categories. James indicates that the basic stuff of the world—and therefore the only rightful candidate for the title "the real"—is a flow of experience, whose parts can be treated in one light so as to give us their mental aspect, from which we further distill the concept of "mind," but in another light can be construed so as to expose their physical side, which by further abstraction gives us the sophisticated concept of "body." The fact that the notions of "mind" and "body" are commonplace in our cultivated thought—rarely taken out and examined or reflected upon—does not make them simple or basic notions at all.[5]

The form of James's answer struck Whitehead strongly, not only in general but in some detail. But there is a marked difference. James apparently wished to sidestep the usual temptations of metaphysics and thereby to exhibit "radical empiricism" or "pragmatism" as a substitute for metaphysics. Whitehead's procedure is to ask why not use the notion of "experience" as itself a basic category of reality, not merely human or animate or sensate reality? "Experience" as a term for the *human* interaction with the world would thus designate only a special *conscious* form of the joint interaction of all entities. Whitehead is very explicit on this deliberately broadened employment of the term: "The way in which one actual entity is qualified by other actual entities is the 'experience' of the actual world enjoyed by that actual entity, as subject" (*PR*, 252). The same notion is repeated in a more complex statement whose vocabulary shows the direct relation to James: "For the purpose of this discussion it is indifferent whether we speak of a 'stream' of experience, or of an 'occasion' of experience. With the former alternative there is togetherness in the stream and with the latter alternative. In either case there is the unique 'experiential togetherness.' " (*PR*, 288). We are reminded of James's term "stream of consciousness," appropriated by literary critics to describe a style of writing, but originally used by James to designate the mental side of the continuity of experience.

Experience, in the ordinary sense of the word, is a complex and conscious case of an interaction that really characterizes all entities; we may correspondingly expect to find universal usages for "mental" and "physical," those derivative aspects of experience which, when taken as both concrete and basic, divide the world into unreconcilable halves. This universalization is exactly what Whitehead undertakes.

The extended terms "physical" and "mental" apply to any actual entity whatsoever, regardless of its complexity. However, "physical" will not mean "inert," nor will "mental" refer to consciousness. The inert entity, like a rock, will prove to be a collection—"society"—of relatively monotonous, repetitive actual entities. And consciousness will be reserved for a high-order mentality of a peculiarly complex sort. Consciousness receives separate treatment in later chapters.[6] What do these terms designate, then, that is common to all actual entities, simple or complex?

To answer the above question, we must begin by observing that every actual occasion has a unique identity all its own, but that it incorporates qualities and characteristics that can be present in other actual entities as well. Even if a very simple actual occasion arises, in which every characteristic quality is related to every other one in exactly the same way as it was in another actual occasion—the nearly ideal monotony in a simple "physical particle" (for example, an electron)—it still has its unique spatiotemporal status. The reality of time means a real actualization that never happened before. Moreover, other actual entities may exactly share the temporal expanse of a given actual entity. Insofar as they do, they are called "contemporaries." Or, at different times different actual entities may occupy the same space as did former actual entities. But spatiality alone or temporality alone is itself a partial abstraction from fundamental spatiotemporality. Spatiotemporality is the primary quantitative feature of an actual entity—and thus no two actual entities are identical in both respects. The situation is much the same as in our normal understanding of bodies—that they may contemporarily occupy different spaces, or that they may occupy the same space of different times, but not the same space *and* time. The difference is that a body is said to be *in* space and time, whereas, strictly speaking, spatiality and temporality—or more concretely, spatiotemporality—are "in" the actual entities which comprise the basic stuff of the world.

Over against this concrete uniqueness of each actual entity, there are certain qualifications of it, characteristics of it, which are not uniquely confined to it. These qualities, which Whitehead calls "eternal objects," have a common feature; they can all "be again." For example, on a submicroscopic scale an electron is an "enduring object" composed of successive actual occasions. Each of these least units in the life of the electron displays charge, mass, and so on, which repeatable characteristics are identical with those of the prior and subsequent actual entities that comprise the enduring object called an "electron." These repeatable elements are *ipso facto* eternal objects, corresponding substantially to what are often called "universals" (*PR*, 76). They are, says Whitehead, the same as Locke's "ideas," for example, " 'whiteness, hardness, sweetness, thinking, motion, man, elephant, army, drunkenness,' and others" (*PR*, 82). The examples given are of macroscopic eternal objects, both simple ("whiteness") and complex ("elephant"). Taken by and in themselves such eternal objects are nowhere. They have no spatiotemporal specificity, as an actual entity does. Indeed, in themselves they are abstract, mere "potentials." They are concrete only insofar as they "ingress" into some actual entity—that is, are embodied in it as characterizing it. Moreover, when an actual occasion comes into being, it is, as we have seen, an instance of self-creation, *causa sui*. But the self-creation is not *ex nihilo*. Rather, the materials for this creative act are delivered to it from past actual occasions in virtue of their being the embodiment of eternal objects which the oncoming actual entity can exploit for its own self-composition. The way is now open to explain the basic difference between the "mental" and "physical" poles of an actual entity.

Any actual entity "feels" or "prehends" past actual entities in two ways, mental and physical. There are correspondingly two fundamental types of "feeling" or "prehending." An actual entity in process of self-construction feels other actual entities as fully concrete—that is, as extended in space-time and as embodying the eternal objects ingredient in it. This concrete taking-account-of is "physical" prehension and is the function of the physical pole. But its composition of itself is selective of eternal objects, which means that it must also be prehending and using eternal objects *qua* eternal objects, abstracted from their particular ingression in the given and completed actual entities. In the case of a higher-order actual entity—say a moment in the conscious life of a thinking person—this process of selection may be of an almost indefinitely intricate sort. At this moment as I write, the whiteness of the paper, the blueness of the ink, the hardness of the desk all enter into my successive acts of consciousness, all but "automatically." But the little marks I make, each of them unique as an achieved act, have an intricate symbolic import far beyond their immediate physical existence, in the abstract realm of repeatable meaning. My consciousness is exploiting this complex realm of meanings in the delicate task of communicating, by minimal means, ideas repeatable in the mind of the reader and repeatable in terms, ultimately, of my own concrete experience. The reader in turn will form his own consciousness partly out of his own past, to which I appeal, and partly from whatever provocation is transferred from the written marks to the multiply reproduced printed page and its closely related marks. Notice here that the emphasis is on *idea,* as a factor in the self-composition of an act of self-consciousness. In my own act there is both the sense of effort and the sense of a mild fatigue. If the prose is obscure, for example, some of the fatigue may be evident. But the self-propelling reader will make his own selection, cutting through that evidence of fatigue imprinted in unattractive prose, to get at the idea, which is the selective target of his concrete effort. The choice is his; his freedom is exemplified in the steadfastness with which he binds himself to his purpose. He is in a very real sense cause of himself, at the point of that effort and in those acts which comprise his thoughts.

"Idea is the object of thinking," says Locke; Whitehead quotes the passage and equates Locke's "ideas" with his own "eternal objects." An eternal object is that which is selected out from the concrete encounter. If we then translate Locke's definition to "Eternal object is the object of thinking," and also hold that eternal objects can be prehended as apart from their given context, we have a helpful clue in understanding how even a very simple actual occasion may be said to have a mental pole. Such mentality will be, of course, far below the level of consciousness; it aims at "prehending" the eternal objects which are ingredient in other actual entities in process of self-making. Where the appropriation of eternal objects by some actual-entity-in-process-of-be-coming is blindly repetitious of the immediate past, the selectivity seems almost preformed and foreordained. It falls into the same pattern as did its immediate ancestors. Here the mental pole is so unadventurous as to be wanting. One time slice in the life of an electron is qualitatively very like the last and the next. Quantitatively it exhibits differences, but these belong to its physical pole. On a macroscopic scale the rock with its uncountable constituents of actual entities all adding up to a massive and repetitious uniformity is so monotonous that we rightly dispose of it for most purposes as "inert," "lifeless," nonmental—that is, as a purely physical entity. We forget the rock may be analyzed as a seething swarm of energetic atomic and subatomic activities which repeat the stability of the world and the fact that these activities *are* acts. Once any actual entity completes its own act of self-creation, it thereby slips into the past. It can hardly reach out of the finished past and cause the present activity, however. The present activity is a new phase in what Whitehead calls the underlying "creativity," which must individuate itself here and now, and always in some relation to the accomplished yet immovable past. Sheer replication of the past in the endurance of unaltering enduring objects is the case of minimal mentality, minimal seizing and using of just those immediate eternal objects of one's immediate parentage. For most practical purposes, we can call this kind of enduring object "physical," in spite of its constituent mental activities. And to the extent that it occurs—in a man or in a rock—the result may well merit the epithet "lifeless," so little of the novel originality of life or mentality is present. "The root fact," says Whitehead,

is that "endurance" is a device whereby an occasion is peculiarly bound

by a single line of physical ancestry, while "life" means
novelty . . . [which leads to the idea] that an organism is "alive" when
in some measure its reactions are inexplicable by *any* tradition of pure
physical inheritance. (*PR*, 159)

He goes on to explain that by "tradition" he means what is ordinarily
called "efficient cause." Yet the freedom is not freedom for its own
sake, nor a sheer disruptive rebellion. It is freedom which is exploited
to give depth and intensity to experience and feeling. "Thus though life
in its essence is the gain of intensity through freedom, yet it can also
submit to canalization and so gain the massiveness of order" (*PR*, 164).

We have now come full circle to our subject. If we are concerned
with what is *alive* we cannot look for "life" among the so-called
ultimate particles of the physical world (whatever science may hold
them to be in any given era of scientific speculation), nor can we
reasonably expect the living thing to be made up of wholly nonliving
things, since then the agglomeration of these particles would be sheerly
accidental. Actually, the quality of being alive is as irreducible and
immediate in the consciousness which apprehends it as anything else in
our experience. Accordingly, we would do well to regard living and
nonliving as matters of degree, thus allowing for some subtlety in our
thought, and incidentally making the broad aspects of the theory of
evolution a bit less mysterious. So also "mentality" and "physicality"
must both belong to the ultimate constitution of things, again as
matters of degree. If we fail to recognize that mentality and physicality
are matters of degree, we may wind up by making minds and bodies so
utterly unlike as to render the relations between them impossible. We
may, that is, fall into the Cartesian gulf. Or, alternatively, we may be
engaged in the futile task of trying to reduce the one to the other, as
has been done by generation after generation of idealists on the one
hand, and of materialists on the other.

(5) *Value and fact.* Another traditional problem which has plagued
philosophers is the relation between values and facts. Facts are often
thought of as self-evident, objective, unalterable. All of these notions
are, however, somewhat vulnerable. The self-evidence of so-called
scientific facts can hardly be seriously maintained at all. For example,
the "scientific" account of matter presents it as being primarily
electromagnetic, though this is not a self-evident feature of matter as

we know it. One might ask, "Is science talking about the reality that lies about us, in our ordinary experience?" The alleged objectivity of facts, if such facts are to be scientifically reported and understood, depends upon the concept of a neutral observer or an observer in a neutral stance. It is to be doubted whether anyone could be wholly neutral and still be an observer. In the first place, he comes to his observation with a set of well-justified categories that have been useful in his previous experience, and he interprets his data, inescapably, at the point of acquiring them. Practical success in the use of common conceptual constructions produces a concept-blindness in which the victim fails to recognize that his very act of observation is interpretative. Even in the intransigent realm of mathematics some concepts are mutable, other dispensable. As a familiar example, the apparently self-evident commutative law for multiplication, so necessary for nondirectional algebras, does not apply to the algebras of vectoral quantities. In physics the classic example of the virtually wholly junked conception of a material ether is another case in point.

We find that values may be as "objective" in one sense of the word as any "facts." For instance, suppose we mean by "objective" "verified by consensus." In the domain of *simple* values, at least, the value of being stuck with a pin or of eating a tender steak will probably get more consensus than we find in red-green colorblindness tests, which are supposed to deal with something factual. Much that passes for "fact" is dubitable, and much that passes for "value" is as "objective" as the apprehension of the color "red." The truth of the matter, as Whitehead sees it, is that all encounter with fact is a processive encounter, never final and never complete. Things that are known are indeed known in relation to the knower. Whitehead insists that there are not two natures, the one perceived in mundane experience and the other thought about in scientific reflection. The living encounter, in the process of interaction, is more basic than the entities *disclosed* in the encounter.

The point about perception and knowledge is that they are never merely factual in their primary content. They can, of course, be bleached and purged of their value-aspects in order to get a tidy realm of systematizable fact, but then the question arises, "How concrete is the purified reality thus obtained?"

Whitehead's procedure is thus not to begin by looking for a basic world of facts which will help us to approach problems of value. Just as he knew that life lurks in the simplest mode of being (as does mentality, however simple and nonconscious), he also realizes that systematically we must begin with value at the root of things or else we may never expect to find it again. Values can hardly be built up of a concatenation of facts. Conversely, there are no pure values. All values and valuations have a coordinate associated aspect of factuality.

The question of fact and value then becomes the question of how those two aspects are co-present in process and how they differ. We have already had some inkling of the answer. Whitehead, in his early career as a philosopher of science, refused to try to develop a philosophy of science which rejects the perceptual facts of the world as part of the primitive data. Analogously, in the mature philosophy, occupied with metaphysics and cosmology generally, he insisted that the value data given in, say, poetry must be accommodated to metaphysics as much as are the observations of scientists, the demands of logicians, and the conclusions of examiners of human behavior.

At first glance, indeed, it seems almost as though he gives priority to that aspect of life which is concerned with its values. 'Value,' he says, "is the word I use for the intrinsic reality of an event" (*SMW*, 136). A stronger statement can hardly be imagined, especially if we couple it with the definition of an actual entity as the limiting type of an event having but one member. At the very heart of reality, it would seem, at the root of reality in its least unit—the actual entity—lies not fact, but value. Moreover, the passage cited is preceded by this: "Remembering the poetic rendering of our concrete experience, we see at once that the element of value, of being valuable, of having value, of being an end in itself, of being something which is for its own sake, must not be omitted in any account of an event as the most concrete actual something."

It is easy to be misled by these remarks. The apparent interpretation seems to be completed by Whitehead's remark that "the actuality is the value" (*SMW*, 155). The difficulty lies in our taking the word "intrinsic" too carelessly. "Intrinsic" normally has an honorific quality about it. As a result "intrinsic reality" sounds like a way of saying "genuine reality" or "*real* reality," but this is not Whitehead's meaning. He means to contrast "intrinsic" with "extrinsic," and he means to make the two modes co-basic as ways of analyzing, or as perspectives upon, reality. It is true that, confronted with the almost inebriate celebration of what is thought to be "objective," Whitehead places the weight of emphasis on the reestablishment of the subjective—or intrinsic—aspect of actuality. He does this, however, by way of correcting an imbalance, and especially in the context of critically evaluating the contributions of the eighteenth and nineteenth centuries to our total world view.[7] It is, of course, *possible* to look at the world as a mere collection of systematizable facts. But, in the first place, we always run the risk of imposing a system rather than of discovering one. Second, the factual aspect of reality is but one aspect and has no unchallengeable status as the root of all being, nor as the primary object of our interest. Indeed, how could a mere fact, devoid of all value, generate any interest? However, the same thing is true of a purely evaluative approach to reality. Since the latter risks are more widely known, Whitehead stresses them less.

Whitehead's meaning for "intrinsic" must be taken with that of "extrinsic" as well. "There is thus," says Whitehead, "an intrinsic and an extrinsic reality of an event, namely, the event as in its own prehension, and the event as in the prehension of other events" (*SMW*, 151). The last phrase, "the event as in the prehension of other events," means "the event as it functions as a relevant entity for apprehension by other actual events." The distinction is a familiar one; it is the distinction between "subjective" and "objective" in one of the many sets of meanings attaching to that pair of terms. From its interior vis-à-vis itself, each actual entity is something "for itself." This is, as we have seen, the root of the conception of the telic, in Whitehead. The telic lies in what he calls the "microscopic meaning" of the "internal process" in each actual entity, through which it "becomes itself." The root notion of efficient causation is that of the "macroscopic meaning" which expresses the "transition from actual entity to actual entity." This corresponds, of course, to the extrinsic reality.

It is in the complex context of our own consciousness that we find familiar data exhibiting the distinction between the extrinsic and the intrinsic realities. We are subjectively aware, on reflection, of how the many aspects of the external world are brought into special relevance for one another, *as they are seen by consciousness itself.* You and I look at the "same" scene. What it signifies, intrinsically, for each of us, depends on how we use it, our own pasts, our future purposes. What you see as an open meadow, rich in natural ecology, I may be envisaging primarily as a potential subdivision. In our respective acts we are not merely passive, we are engaged in self-creation as well, by the way in which we apprehend what is external to us.

Such acts and the series of such acts, generate an aspect of reality as "actual" as any other aspect. In their innermost "intrinsic" nature they pose a problem for communication. Poetry is at least partly an effort to breach the communicative barrier. For this task "objective" language is too puny. In any case, difficulties in communication can hardly constitute a test for the real. Whitehead's point is that the root of value lies in such "innerness," whether it be of that complex and high-order mentality which exhibits self-consciousness or in the simple and limited privacy of very elementary actual entities. All other value is derivative, for not until something becomes a value for itself can it function as a value for something else.

The consciousness of value begins with self-valuing. For example, Whitehead says, "The moment of religious consciousness starts from self-valuation, but it broadens into the concept of the world as a realm of adjusted values, mutually intensifying or mutually destructive. (*RM*, 59).

At the same time, there is an intransigent objectivity in what occurs, however it may be construed by various subjects. "A primrose by the river's brim" may be just a primrose "and nothing more." But it can be nothing less, either. There is evidently a common denominator of factuality, extrinsicality, "objectivity" if you like, in the world-process, which constitutes a limit on the plasticity of the world. I am at liberty to make of the primrose an occasion for the soaring of my soul, or the starting point for an elegant poetic figure. And what I do with it is as real as what it "is" (as sheer object) to be done with. But I cannot make it into a yellow lizard or a hot potato.

At issue is how concretely one wishes to view the world. We often tend to regard the world very abstractly, for the purpose of getting some particular result. "I hold," says Whitehead, "that philosophy is the critic of abstractions" (*SMW*, 126). He exemplifies the same point when, in speaking of enduring objects (that is, complexes of actual entities, where there is a sustained repetition of pattern with novel elements in some kind of orderly synthesis), he says:

There is, thus, in this event a memory of the antecedent life-history of its own dominant pattern, as having formed an element of value in its own antecedent environment. This concrete prehension, from within, of the life-history of an enduring fact is analysable into two abstractions, of which one is the enduring entity which has emerged as a real matter of fact to be taken account of by other things, and the other is the individualised embodiment of the underlying energy of realisation. (*SMW,* 153-54)

This passage introduces three notions which we have not yet explored, but will shortly: (1) the organization of least units of reality, "actual entities," into the groups of "enduring objects" of ordinary experience; (2) the "underlying activity," called the "creativity" in *Religion in the Making* and *Process and Reality;* and (3) "prehension." The point of the passage, as included here, is that what is true for the individual actual entity singly is true for those complexes of actual entities which corporately comprise the persistent things in the world; they have an intrinsicality, an interiority, however minimal. This intrinsicality is the foundation of their internal order or "pattern," as well as of their extrinsic "objective" availability to other enduring objects which take account of them, each in its own—that is, subjective—way. Whitehead's point is that exclusive attention to either feature is an "abstraction" and is therefore, philosophically, a failure, whatever else its usefulness.

In summary, then, "extrinsic" and "intrinsic" designate the same basic modes of analysis as do "factual" and "valuational," "efficient cause" and "telic cause," and finally "objective" and "subjective," respectively. Moreover, in many ways, the same distinction is to be found in the familiar "physical" and "mental." This subject will be investigated in greater detail in Chapter 3.

(6) *Creativity, Freedom, Novelty.* Whitehead's doctrine of temporality leads to his conception of creativity and vice versa. In general, basic notions in a speculative philosophy require one another, that is, can not be explicated apart from one another. Whitehead calls this their "coherence." He says:

"Coherence," as here employed, means that the fundamental ideas, in terms of which the scheme is developed, presuppose each other so that in isolation they are meaningless. This requirement does not mean that they are definable in terms of each other; it means that what is indefinable in one such notion cannot be abstracted from its relevance to the other notions. It is the ideal of speculative philosophy that its fundamental notions shall not seem capable of abstraction from each other. (*PR*, 5)

What is true of the fundamental notions of speculative philosophy is also true of the nature of the world it seeks to expose. Whitehead continues the passage above as follows:

In other words, it is presupposed that no entity can be conceived in complete abstraction from the system of the universe, and that it is the business of speculative philosophy to exhibit this truth. This character is its coherence.

The *specula* is therefore a tower from which one gains a superior per*spec*tive, where relations among entities are seen to be multiple and mutually signifying. In brief: the weblike character of reality requires a structurally similar weblike interdependence of basic notions to describe it.[8] The reader will notice that the organization of the present book follows Whitehead's insistence on the necessity of repeatedly recurring to basic notions.

Three such basic notions exhibit an unusual degree of coherence, and all three arise from a consideration of temporality: creativity, freedom, novelty. In the above discussion of temporality, the subject glossed over was that of *temporal novelty*.

According to some thinkers, the passage of time is primarily a subjective phenomenon. This view is held by such widely diverse speculators as Saint Augustine, whose eyes were fixed on deity and eternity,[9] and Hermann Weyl, who has persuaded himself that "The objective world simply is, it does not happen."[10] But if we regard time as an objective phenomenon, then "before" and "after" refer to a fundamental reality, and there must thus be novelty in the universe. No matter how much the present repeats the past in however many ways, the present never was before and never will be, in its full concreteness, again.

Whitehead's position on this point is interesting. One cannot say that he *postulates* this idea, for he never flatly states it at all. Nor can one say that he draws it as a result or conclusion, for no argument is given. He employs it implicitly again and again as a presupposition for all talk of creativity and freedom. The conception of the uniqueness of each passing moment is virtually deducible from the proposition that *process* is reality. Process is inherently temporal or it is nothing. Whitehead's defense of this notion is in his constant reasonable use of it to render systematically clear—but not distorted—certain aspects of our experience. As Whitehead says, in conclusion of his own introduction to this subject of the "production of novelty," "The sole appeal is to intuition" (*PR*, 32). At the present level of analysis, we may translate "intuition" as that which is immediately given, an irreducible element in our experience, concretely familiar to everyone, difficult to convey (by its very nature), yet not capable of being explained away.

In summary thus far, we may say that "creativity," "novelty," and "freedom" are terms requiring one another for even elementary speculation. They "cohere" in the above-mentioned sense, coherence being the rule of reality and of any system that undertakes to expose such a reality. And collectively they derive their coherence from and explicate the basic supposition of the reality of time as in passage.

The fundamental notion from the point of view of a system is "creativity." Whitehead's first systematic thoughts on this subject arose in the context of a work on the philosophy of religion, the processive implications of whose title is worth mention: *Religion in the Making.* He says in this work:

The temporal world and its formative elements constitute for us the all-inclusive universe.

These formative elements are:

1. The creativity whereby the actual world has its character of temporal passage to novelty.

2. The realm of ideal entities, or forms, which are in themselves not actual, but are such that they are exemplified in everything that is actual, according to some proportion of relevance.

3. The actual but non-temporal entity whereby the indetermination of mere creativity is transmuted into a determinate freedom. This non-temporal actual entity is what men call God—the supreme God of rationalized religion. (*RM*, 90)

Of these three "formative" elements, the first is the subject in hand, creativity. The second, "the realm of ideal entities or forms," is the realm of "eternal objects," whose members we have encountered (in Section 4) already. These are the possible qualifications of events which are actualized by actual entities. The third formative element, God, should be noted for its peculiarity, namely, that although it is actual it is nontemporal. This, on the face of it, seems contradictory, and must also fall into a larger, separate discussion (see below, Section 8). Our present concern is with the notion of creativity.

In undertaking to understand the notion of creativity, we are beginning with the fundamental level of actuality, viewed as dynamic. Telicly the world must be understood in terms of deity; structurally it must be understood in terms of the extensive continuum, spatiotemporality, and its qualitative elements, "ideal entities" or "eternal objects." But as to its "ongoingness," its "drive," we must consider its creativity. Why, for example, should one actual entity come into being after another? For any occurrence to be complete, it must be just that—complete, over, done with. Definiteness means closure. For example, closed definiteness is a prerequisite for a completed act of observation. This "objectified" world, however, is always in process of outrunning itself. The "ongoingness" is unending. Even our commonplace immediate perception is perception of a set of occurrences whose very observability relegates them to the immediate past. Pervasively present in every act of perceptual encounter, however, we have, in addition to the qualitative aspects of our perception, the inescapable sense of the passage of time. Every action we take, even those apparently not willed, and especially those which lie deep in the automation of habit, can only be finally understood as having an ingredient of anticipation. This anticipation is of a world incomplete, in some way open, unactualized, not yet come. We at once perceive a closed world of definite fact and sense, an open world of anticipation, coming toward us by way of a temporality not yet elapsed. To put the point in terms of the blurred boundary between the living and the nonliving: no completely dead and finished past has—by definition—any ingredient in it which would justify the existence of the present or the onrush of the future.

Even in a would-be rigid determination, the notion of the past as *causing* the present has implicit recourse to this notion of creativity.

The past cause can hardly be wholly "gone" and yet be an ingredient in the present activity before us. The more that scientific explanation has aimed at limiting explanation to efficient causation, the more embarrassing this problem has become. A materialistic mechanism may invoke the notion of a designing deity who created the spatiotemporal world, placed its material creatures in the world, and gave them their initial shove. Or it may turn its back on origins, and shruggingly point out that we have trouble enough following what happens without asking about "Where does the energy come from?" Yet the fact that the present is active and open, while the past is closed and inactive, remains. How are they conjoined? Aristotle developed the notion of a Prime Mover in almost exclusively telic terms: that toward which all things are drawn, each according to the limits of its nature. Current "cosmologists" (as the term is used by astronomers) vacillate between a "big bang" theory of the origin of the universe, in which all energy is the outcome of a single primeval explosion dying away ultimately into a dead-level entropy, and an "eternalist" doctrine in which the constant dissipation of energy is balanced by a spontaneous generation of it, the so-called hydrogen-cloud theory. But creativity remains a problem.

What is most significant in this creativity is its quality of formlessness. As Whitehead says, "This protean character of the creativity forbids us from conceiving it as an actual entity. For its character lacks determinateness" (*RM*, 92). We are not to think of the creativity as sheer raw energy—of whatever sort—however. The creativity is not separable from its creatures. "Thus the creatures remain with the creativity. . . . For the temporal world is an essential incompleteness" *(ibid.).* "Creature" is here used as a synonym for "actual occasion" (*RM*, 91) and therefore for any *temporal* actual entity. The emphasis is on the temporal transition from the accomplished past to the present-still-in-process-of-formation. "It has not the character of a definite matter of fact, such as attaches to an event in past history, viewed from a present standpoint" (*RM*, 92).

Whitehead develops the conception of creativity still further in *Process and Reality* and relates it to the third of the "formative" elements in the earlier work. "In the philosophy of organism this ultimate is termed 'creativity.'. . ." (*PR*, 11). We postpone the notion of deity until Section 8; we note in passing that the temporal dynamic is *from* creativity, so to speak, and *toward* God, viewed as a primordial being. In this respect, the primordial nature of God is like Aristotle's Prime Mover, not so much a source of motion (in the broad Greek sense) as its "lure," to use a favorite Whiteheadian expression.

In the early part of *Process and Reality,* Whitehead begins the whole system of categories with the notion of creativity. In the "category of the ultimate," the notions "many," "one," and "creativity" "cohere" in the sense already indicated and in the most intimate way: no one of them can be in any way approached by itself. "One" is not a mathematical notion here but something which denotes "singularity"—the kind of singularity which each actual entity has, that it is just itself. "Many" denotes the universe conceived as a multiplicity of such singularities. "Creativity" then refers to the unification of many diverse aspects of the universe, each of them relevant in some way, into each unique actual occasion. Whitehead writes, "Creativity . . . is that ultimate principle by which the many, which are the universe disjunctively, become the one actual occasion, which is the universe conjunctively" (*PR,* 31). One may reasonably ask if it is not a little crowded inside the actual occasion if it has somehow got a bit of everything else in it. But the point (to be developed in Chapter 3) is that relevance may be negative relevance, *exclusion.* Moreover, we are not to think of inclusion as some kind of spatial enclosure. Characteristics of an actual occasion are relational. They are not qualities all bottled up in some precise space.

Whitehead repeatedly compares "creativity" to Aristotle's "primary substance" or "matter" (*PR,* 32, 46, 47). It is that from which all that is definite appears, but its potentialities constantly outrun any particular actualization. The "outrunning" is the passage of "time," properly the "temporal passage." The *continuous* passage of time can thus be understood as the *continuous* realization of these possibilities. And the possibilities are nothing other than eternal objects, either as actualized in accomplished fact or as nonactualized, or both.

The creativity includes, therefore, the definite creatures which partially embody it. But it passes beyond them, proteanly, always expressing itself in new actual occasions which are nevertheless limited by what has already gone before. Creativity is thus "the principle of novelty" (*PR,* 31), expressing itself in the appearance of new temporal creatures.

It remains to show what the creativity has to do with freedom. Clearly, if freedom means self-determination, then every actual entity is an instance of freedom, insofar as it is *causa sui,* self-creating. "The freedom inherent in the universe is constituted by this element of self-causation" *(PR,* 135). Yet an actual occasion creates itself out of the past, that is, *creatures* which "remain with the creativity." This is not a *creatio ex nihilo,* then, but one that must conform to what the past is. Such " 'decided' conditions are never such as to banish freedom inherent in the universe is constituted by this element of circle to the conception of life, where we began. "Life," says Whitehead, "is a bid for freedom: an enduring entity binds any one of its occasions to the line of its ancestry" *(PR,* 159). The "enduring" entity is a complex of actual occasions which displays internal pattern and coherence, so that the composing actual entities have special relevance for one another, along a time line. The subject of "life" reintroduces the distinction between physical and mental prehension. This subject in turn includes still another through which we have passed: the contrast between "efficient" and "final" cause. The passage quoted above continues shortly with an extraordinarily rich statement which brings together the ideas of *freedom, novelty, life, mentality, physicality,* and *"final"* and *"efficient" cause:* "The root fact is," says Whitehead, continuing the account of an "enduring entity,"

that "endurance" is a device whereby an occasion is peculiarly bound by a single line of physical ancestry, while "life" means novelty. . . . What has to be explained is originality of response to stimulus. This amounts to the doctrine that an organism is "alive" when in some measure its reactions are inexplicable by *any* tradition of pure physical inheritance.
Explanation by "tradition" is merely another phraseology for explanation by "efficient cause." We require explanation by "final cause." Thus a single occasion is alive when the subjective aim which determines its process of concrescence has introduced a novelty of definiteness not to be found in the inherited data of its primary phase. The novelty is introduced conceptually . . . [i.e., by a prehension or grasping issuing from the "mental pole" of an actual occasion]. *(PR,* 159)

The freedom is always there, in its preconditioned form, in the sheer advance of creative novelty. The question is, to put it quite simply, what does the oncoming actual occasion do with its opportunities? If it merely reproduces, in a limited way, the patterns of its immediate spatiotemporal past, including those eternal objects which its ancestors did, and in the selfsame way, then the reproduction is almost entirely physical, hardly deserving the term "life" and confining its own birthright of novelty to its spatiotemporal uniqueness. *In short, if an enduring object, like a stone or a small physical particle, is composed of strings or webs of actual occasions which are the sheerest repetition throughout the passage of new time, the ordinary designation of them as "lifeless" is of great practical advantage and very close to true. The same is true of, say, a cliff, whose changes are easily referred to external agencies having little or nothing to do with the cliff itself. To the extent that there is novelty, then, some grasped eternal object has been exploited in a way different from what has gone before, the "mental" pole has been distinctly operative, and the sheer physical inheritance is inadequate to account for the structure of the actual reason in question. To this same extent life is present, and "life is a bid for freedom."*

To complete the swift sketch of Whitehead's philosophy, we turn to the remaining two formative elements: the ideal forms (eternal objects) and God.

(7) *Form, Ideal Forms, Eternal Objects.* From the time of Plato to the present a question has plagued philosophers and, to some extent, thoughtful laymen. In one way or another it constituted one of the three or four basic controversies in the Middle Ages, where it sometimes assumed a pivotal role. The question may be stated this way: do the things that recur in nature, and/or thought, have a separate existence, and indeed may they be said to exist at all? Think of the rectangle, say, that of an Athenian bench, long since crumbled—or again, think of the rectangular field not far way in the present. Rectangularity is present in the books, the desk, and the very sheet of paper I write on also. Rectangles are found in many places, at many times. What of rectangular*ity,* which as such is a mathematical object occupying no particular time or space and yet displaying logically invariant characteristics? These characteristics are always and everywhere the same for me, an ancient Greek, or a modern freshman. Rectangular things exist; surely rectangularity exists, but in what sense?

Plato leans, it seems, toward holding that the timeless forms of things—both mathematical "forms," like triangularity and fourness (present in all quadrangles) and true forms, such as justice, difference, unity, and so on—exist eternally unchanging, in a realm all their own, that of "being." The changing world of perception, called "becoming," is the scene of a constant mixture of rough practical exemplifications of these timeless and essential forms.

During the Middle Ages some philosophers insisted that these "universals" or "forms" existed only conceptually, not in actuality. Thus they were available as separable objects of thought, but not in reality. Other philosophers, called "nominalists," said that universals "exist" only insofar as they are embodied in the concrete world; otherwise their existence is only "nominal," that of a name. In general the "conceptualists" had the stronger position. A strict nominalist would always be under embarrassment if asked to explain mathematics. It is very easy to show what the angle between adjacent sides of a regular polygon of 1,163 sides is—and not only *is*, but *must be.* It seems unlikely that we have instances of such polygons; yet we can say with certainty what some of their properties *would be,* if there were any such. Existence of such a nature seems to be more than nominal.

Whitehead's undertaking here is to look at the problem perhaps more broadly than any philosopher before him. As he sees it, there is not a simple question of space-and-time-filling things versus absolutely reliable but non-spatiotemporal things. We do not have just two orders of existence. Not only must both kinds of things be said to exist, but many other types as well which do not fall into either classification. There are, in all, eight categories of existence, and they, like other cohering concepts, must be understood, not in isolation, but in relation to one another.

I shall list these categories here, with brief accounts of each, to provide the immediate context for the "existence" of ideal forms in their Whiteheadian presentation, namely as "Eternal objects."

(i) Actual Entities. We have already encountered these.

(ii) Prehensions. Whitehead also calls them "Concrete Facts of Relatedness" and "feelings." They are, as their name suggests, graspings of other actual entities. Collectively these prehensions comprise the "stuff" of an actual entity as it creates itself.

(iii) Nexūs (sing. "nexus"). Whitehead dubs these "Public Matters of Fact." They are the complexes of more or less closely associated actual entities which include the more obvious "enduring objects" of common experience.

(iv) Subjective Forms. Whitehead also calls these "Private Matters of Fact." This is the way a feeling or prehension is felt. If I hear a note of music, that is a prehension of a world other than my sheerly personal moment of physical consciousness. In its context the prehension brings to me composer, performer, instrument, and so on. But the special way in which this note is grasped here and now, including my own emotions on hearing it, are its subjective form (*PR*, 346-53). Subjective form, says Whitehead, "in abstraction from the feeling is merely a complex eternal object" (*PR*, 356).

(v) Eternal objects. Pure possibilities for the qualification of an actual entity. Roughly: characteristics or properties of actualities.

(vi) Propositions. A thorny subject, even for the advanced sutdent. Speaking simply, a proposition is a hybrid. In a categorical proposition, "Sam's cat is brown," "Sam's cat" designates a nexus composed of highly interconnected actual entities. "Brown" is an eternal object. Since the proposition, to be one, must be meaningful, "Sam's cat" must refer to a real actuality. But since the proposition is a proposition whether it is true or false, the predicate "brown" designates only a legitimate possibility. Eternal objects taken in abstraction are nothing but possibilities. So a proposition, as such, has one foot in actuality, the other in possibility.

(vii) Multiplicities. Roughly: collections considered in their diversity from one another. Whitehead says that strictly speaking a "multiplicity" is not a "proper entity" at all, therefore (*PR*, 44-45).

(viii) Contrasts. A very complex subject, not fully developed in *Process and Reality*, and only lightly commented upon in this book. A quotation from Whitehead will give us some help, however:

The most obvious examples of a contrast are to be found by confining attention purely to eternal objects. The contrast between blue and red cannot be repeated as *that* contrast between any other pair of colours, or any pair of sounds, or between a colour and a sound. (*PR*, 349)

"Among these eight categories of existence," says Whitehead, "actual entities and eternal objects stand out with a certain extreme finality. The other types of existence have a certain intermediate character" (*PR*, 33). The first part of this statement is an acknowledgment of the reasonableness of the history of a controversy which has dealt with the problem of universals and particulars as if they were the *only* modes of existence. We tend to divide the world up into what is temporal in its inmost nature, and what is not, then undertake to decide whether both aspects may be said to "exist" or only one. Much as Kant reacted to isolated problems about substance (as in Locke) and cause (as in Hume), Whitehead reacts to the questions about the "existence" of universals versus the "existence" of individual things. Kant placed the two categories of "substance" and "cause" in a larger scheme of twelve categories and dealt with the categoreal problem directly, thus exhibiting the roles played by two of the more controversial categories. Whitehead's discernment of eight categories of existence is analogous. The question, then, is not "What exists?" but "What are the ways in which different types of existence are related?"

For Whitehead eternal objects are called "eternal" because they are transtemporal. That is, the passage of time does not affect their natures. Further, they are called "objects" for several reasons. (1) In the first place, their natures as sheer possibilities for "concretion" depend not at all upon their being so concreted, or having "ingressed" into an actual occasion. They are what they are, regardless of exemplification or instantiation. (2) *A fortiori* they are what they are, regardless of being apprehended in anyone's consciousness. They are not generated by mentality. Their individuality and their relations to one another are invariant. (3) But the most important sense in which they are objects is that, as qualifications of an actual occasion, they *objectify* that actual occasion; they provide objectivity, in the sense of objecthood. They are the eternal objects by means of which an actual occasion is a unit in an enduring object.

It is thus with some curiosity that we learn there are eternal objects of two main species, "subjective" and "objective." These will be identified here and commented upon later. Those of the "objective species" are "the mathematical Platonic forms." They give the actual entity its own objectivity and definiteness. The "subjective species" include such things as "an emotion, or an intensity, or an adversion, or a pleasure, or a pain." This is an objectification of the actual entity *for* a percipient, generally, one would suppose, as that actual entity is a member of a nexus (*PR*, 446).

Subjective eternal objects, then, include such things as "red" (*PR*,

447). We must here pass over the question that automatically arises: how does Whitehead escape falling into the hole which Locke did not see, the arbitrary division of the world into primary and secondary qualities? It must be admitted that there is a great gap in Whitehead's doctrine of eternal objects and that he never provided more than very minimal clues for filling in the gap.

We may expect that the varieties of eternal objects are countless, and that they must be stratifiable as to degree of complexity. In *Science and the Modern World* eternal objects are exemplified much as in the later work, in terms of shape and color.[11] There is thus a least grade of eternal objects called "the grade of zero complexity" (*SMW*, 240). The first level of complexity above this will be sets of possible relations among the eternal objects of zero complexity. Three colors may be related to one another—in actuality—as the faces of a tetrahedron. This abstract possibility (we remember that all eternal objects, examined in isolation, are nothing but possibles) constitutes a complex eternal object, of grade one. Further complexification may or may not have reference to this complex eternal object. The fact that such possible relations hold among simple (grade zero) eternal objects is itself a fact within the realm of eternal objects. In the example just given it lies in the relational essence of an eternal object that it bear innumerable possible relations to others. Indeed, as one thinks about these eternal objects, there is some doubt whether any simple eternal object could ingress into an actual entity, solely by itself. Over against its relational essence, the eternal object has an individual essence, its own nature, whether simple or complex. Whitehead evidently means to be using the term "essence" in its classical sense of "whatness," "quiddity." In the case of a simple eternal object this will be the sheer quality, say a particular shade of green. In the case of a complex eternal object, the qualitative identity of the eternal object will be *analyzable,* but that does not destroy its integrity, its uniqueness. For example, the same three colors could be represented on a tetrahedron in several ways. Each of these ways, as a *possible,* is a separate, *different* eternal object of the first grade of complexity, although each of them, on analysis, reduces to the same set of eternal objects of zero complexity.

We come now to what was called above the "gap." We are given simple eternal objects, colors, shapes, sounds, and so forth—called "sensa" in *Process and Reality* (174 ff.)—and we are given very complex ones as well: man, drunkenness (*PR*, 82), and very little in between. Yet we are told that there is a continuously ascending degree of complexity in the realm of eternal objects. Evidently it soon passes out of the realm of the immediately sensible, although being analyzable to what is sensible. We will take a closer look at eternal objects in a later chapter, and something of the general *structure* of that realm can be investigated. But this closer look will not give us much guidance about the *contents* of the realm of eternal objects. The problem has existed since Plato's time. In the *Republic,* justice is said to be a form present in all just things. There is no necessary sensory overlap between justice as embodied in a law and justice as embodied in a just man or his acts. Yet in each case we encounter the justice by means of our senses. How and to what extent does the sensory ingression of simple eternal objects grade over into the complex ingression of complex eternal objects whose *unity* is revealed only to reflection, rather than to inspection? Whitehead specifically says of both eternal objects and actual occasions that they are "unfathomable in their variety of type" (*SMW*, 251). We cannot expect even a list of ascending strata of complexity, nor should we. Nonetheless, transition from the presented eternal object to the *intellected* one is of real concern for the theory of mentality.

(8) *God.* God is the last of the three formative elements given in *Religion in the Making.* He is an actual entity, but a nontemporal one; all other actual entities are temporal, actual *occasions.* God conceived as nontemporal does not mean God as out of time. For example, Whitehead says, in the same study: "The inclusion of God in every creature shows itself in the determination whereby a definite result is emergent" (*RM,* 94). The question is: What "temporality" of actual occasions does God *not* have while He is yet included in every (temporal) creature?

The thing about the temporality of any entity which Whitehead wishes to exclude from God's nature is *transiency.* A temporal entity is such that there was a time when it did not exist; it comes into existence and it perishes, becoming "objectively immortal." Where temporality means "finite and limited in the temporal order of things" God is nontemporal. But since He is included in every (temporal) creature, He is obviously temporal in the sense of being imminent in temporal passage. Briefly, Whitehead is talking about an "everlasting" God, God understood as being co-present, at every "present time," in the birth of each creature.

This can be better understood in the context of three theological problems: the Problem of Evil, the Problem of Freedom, the Problem of Immortality.

The Problem of Evil. Whitehead's thoughts on this familiar problem may be subtly developed, but they are not subtle in their foundations. If God be all-powerful, then it would seem that all that exists owes its origins to Him. God then appears as the author of evil, and His Goodness now seems not only inexplicable, but perhaps not even possible. Whitehead puts the point neatly:

> Among medieval and modern philosophers, anxious to establish the religious significance of God, an unfortunate habit has prevailed of *paying to Him metaphysical compliments. He has been conceived as the foundation of the metaphysical situation with its ultimate activity.* If this conception be adhered to, there can be no alternative except to discern in Him the origin of all evil as well as of all good. (*SMW*, 258; italics mine)

Since God's nature is the final author and provoker of good, his all-powerfulness, especially as creator, must be sacrificed. Such widely diverse authors as Royce and Kierkegaard have argued that apparent evil is only the shortness of the vision in recognizing the Grand Design, or the love that passeth human understanding. But then one may wonder why man was brought to earth with such defective vision. Others with a streak, or more, of mysticism, have held that evil is a relativity between greater and lesser goods. Undoubtedly, this notion has an exemplary effect when used by persons against themselves caught in the act of feeling sorry for themselves. As a subjective correction it can be defended, at least in terms of the results it gets. But what of the burned child crying alone and dying in a ruined city? As an objective category, evil conceived as a differential between goods is harder to support.

Whitehead takes neither of the above tacks. Nor does he take still another view, the Manichean view that the world is the scene of a great battle between the powers of Good and those of Evil. Over against God there stands an independent power, it is true. But it is the first "formative element," creativity. In the passage underscored above, it is called the "ultimate activity." This creativity is the temporal surge which, while including its creatures, constantly erupts into new creatures, or rather *through* new creatures, using its power to create them against and from the background of the past. Such eruptivity easily becomes *dis*ruptivity, when the creatures that emerge are in conflict with one another. "There is evil when things are at cross purposes" (*RM,* 97). But the creativity which stands over against God's nature simply *is;* it is neither good nor evil. Even "chaos is not to be identified with evil; for harmony requires the due coordination of chaos, vagueness, narrowness, and width" (*PR,* 171). However, "insistence on birth at the wrong season is the trick of evil" (*PR,* 341). God's task, everlastingly present in the temporal world, but not passing with it, is the realization of value. "The purpose of God is the attainment of value in the temporal world" (*RM,* 100).

The Problem of Freedom. Closely connected with the foregoing is the problem of freedom, this time in a broader context than when we encountered it before. Freedom has two aspects. Freedom *from* generally looks to the past. The condition of this negative freedom is that of creativity, which in its restless "forward" drive outruns its own creatures and emerges in the development and concretion of new ones. As felt, we have called this drive "temporality." As thought about, reflectively and abstractly considered, apart from its qualitative features, we may call it "time" or perhaps "the passage of time." But positive freedom looks to the future, is a freedom *for.* Whitehead says that life is a "bid for freedom" and explains, as we saw above, that life is present to just the degree that the novel temporality is qualitatively embodied in actual occasions, so that former actual occasions do not represent the sole source of patterning to be found in the present actual occasion.

Where does this new pattern, or newness in and of the pattern (of eternal objects ingredient in the actual occasion) "come from"? Strictly speaking, it comes from, in the sense of being concreted and actualized by it, the actual occasion itself, which is *causa sui.* It also "comes from" the past, which is a constant limitation of the present, yet is nonetheless the inlet of raw materials from which the actual occasion creates itself. Freedom is the opportunity that an actual occasion has for using *its* past in *its* own way. And all of this "coming from" is but a restatement of two of the three "formative elements," creativity and eternal objects. We may guess that there is a sense in which the novelty of pattern "comes from" God, also. This is so.

But now what happens to freedom? For, once Deity appears against the background of the Judaeo-Christian tradition of all-powerfulness, then human freedom seems to vanish. Who and what can be other than God made him—or it? We have come upon another aspect, in the context of the subject of Freedom, of Whitehead's insistence that God is not the sole author of all that is. "It is important for my argument," Whitehead says, "to insist upon the unbounded freedom within which the actual is a unique categorical determination" (*SMW*, 253). The same theme is repeated in a work devoted primarily to religion: "If we trace the evil in the world to the determinism derived from God, then the inconsistency in the world is derived from the consistency of God" (*RM*, 99).

God is not boundless in His power; He is not the author of evil, nor is the creativity, for it is the condition of both good and evil. "Good" and "evil" are meaningful terms only as they designate the actual (not the creativity, which insofar as it is "protean" undergirds the actual).[12] "Value," says Whitehead, "is inherent in actuality itself" (*RM*, 100). Moreover, "There is no such thing as bare value. There is always a specific value, which is the created unit of feeling arising out of the specific mode of concretion of the diverse elements" (*RM*, 103). Every concretion is the achievement of some value. In this respect, Whitehead is somewhat like those neo-Platonists who equate degrees of being with degrees of goodness. However, the neo-Platonists regard evil as a sheer differential, a negativity between positivities. Whitehead rejects this view: "Evil is positive and destructive; what is good is positive and creative" (*RM*, 96). Indeed in a way evil is itself a (temporally limited) good. "Evil, triumphant in its enjoyment, is so far good in itself; but beyond itself it is evil in its character of a destructive agent among things greater than itself" (*RM*, 95).

The problem of evil and that of freedom are closely knit together. God's goodness is unlimited; His power is not. If God's power were in all respects unlimited, we should then have no freedom of individual things—actual occasions—and hence no freedom of persons. Moreover,

God would be creative of evil as well as of good, if all that is, owed its origins to God. Yet God is a "formative element." What is His role in the becoming of an actual occasion, then? His purpose is the "attainment of value in the temporal world." How is it done?

The answer to the above question, stripped to a dangerous simplification, is that in God's nature there lie all the possibilities, subject to many types of limitation, for any future patterns of eternal objects that might be actualized. Even more briefly: *the realm of eternal objects lies in God's nature.* We recall that this is merely a realm of the possible, insofar as we conceive it apart from actuality. When a new actual occasion exhibits its freedom, in the form of a *qualitative* novelty, it has "chosen" from the realm of the possible, already present in God's nature, a set of eternal objects interrelated in such a way that they can be actualized, that is, rendered concrete. But this "choice" is not coerced. It is the response to a "lure." "He is the lure for feeling, . . . the initial 'object of desire' . . . [and insofar very like Aristotle's unmoved mover]" (*PR*, 522-23). God is the "goal towards novelty" (*PR*, 135). "Apart from the intervention of God, there could be nothing new in the world, and no order in the world" (*PR*, 377). By reason of God conceived as "primordial actuality," "there is an order in the relevance of eternal objects to the process of creation" (*PR*, 522). This aspect is but one way of looking at God. Whitehead calls it the "Primordial Nature of God." It helps to anatomize the word "primordial" here into "prime" and "order." The realm of eternal objects is a realm of types of possible order among possibles. It is prime, that is, first. Such order, to come into actuality, must first have been *possible.*

The other principal way of looking at Deity is in the "Consequent Nature." The realm of eternal objects as lying in God's nature gives us only the inactive possibilities which constitute a "lure." But God is an *act*ual entity as well. We have seen that His nontemporality means his character of not passing with passing time. Such everlastingness (see *PR*, 524), which is an immanence in all that comes into being, coupled with the fact that the process of coming into being is open-ended, constantly adding to itself, means that the consequent nature of God is also open-ended, incomplete (*ibid.*). God so conceived is a conserver of all that comes into being, permitting the readjustment of values beyond the brief temporality of any finite actual occasion. "He saves the world as it passes into the immediacy of his own life" (*PR*, 525). Whitehead repeatedly uses the word "tender" or "tenderly" for this action of God, and specifically says that God "does not create the world, he saves it: or, more accurately, he is the poet of the world, with tender patience leading it by his vision of truth, beauty, and goodness" (*PR*, 526). Speaking in more metaphysical and less emotional terms, "The 'consequent nature' of God is the physical prehension by God of the actualities of the evolving universe" (*PR*, 134).

The consequent nature of God receives a fuller treatment in Chapter 9. Here it has brought us to the third theological problem, that of immortality: "The consequent nature of God is the fluent world become 'everlasting' by its objective immortality in God" (*PR*, 527).

The Problem of Immortality. Once again we are returned to questions of time and temporality. What is the status of the past? Strictly speaking, it has been stripped of active agency, although its completedness determines what possibilities are available for realization, for actualization. The answer given above is that it has become "objectively immortal." Such objectivity is through and through physical, however. As we have just seen, God's consequent nature at least begins with the "physical prehension . . . of the actualities of the evolving universe."

The doctrine of immortality, customarily relegated with sectarian swiftness to the realm of the spiritual, is here in Whitehead at least founded in the realm of the physical. For Whitehead it will not do to abolish a Cartesian dualism in metaphysics, only to reestablish it in philosophy of religion or in theology. The basic consideration is, of course, that although God is different from all other actual entities in his nontemporality, he is like them in having a dipolar nature, both physical and mental (*PR*, 524). Just as Whitehead did not suppose we can generate the purely mental out of the purely physical (either in actual fact or in speculation), nor the living from that which is utterly unalive, nor value wholly separate from fact, so also he does not suppose that immortality is a doctrine of immateriality alone. Immortality is rooted fast in its most obvious form, physical immortality.

This insight amounts to one of Whitehead's most singular contributions to a metaphysics of theology. It amounts to a recognition that the intuition of Death and Transfiguration lies before us in the commonplaces of our experience of passing time. Driven from this, its natural foundation (as so many primitive religions show), it becomes a remote and weird notion, likely to be tossed aside by persons of matter-of-fact mentality. In Whitehead's behalf we may ask, "What is the striking power of a religious doctrine which stretches and sophisticates its conceptions so far that they don't square practically with the gross features of ordinary experience at all?"

Immortality begins with actual occasions, in their full physicality.

CHAPTER 3

The Biography of an Actual Occasion

Whitehead's differences from the philosophical traditions of the past are convincingly summarized in his conception of an actual occasion. A complete elaboration of this doctrine would not only repeat his own analysis but would go beyond it. Even Whitehead's masterpiece, *Process and Reality,* is incomplete on the subject of actual occasions, sometimes on what seem to be quite fundamental issues. An actual occasion is multifariously dual, both mental and physical, both coming to be and perishing, both a unity and a diversity, and so on. The effort to analyze the actual occasion is an undertaking in sheer logical conception that has few antecedents. "The" actual occasion analyzed here will often have to be a much more complicated model than is necessary for many examples, in order to include all cases.

I *The Analysis of Passage*

The fundamental *fact* of passage is the appearance of temporal novelty, of the coming into being of what never was before and never will be again, a precipitation of a set of eternal objects with just this set of spatiotemporal coordinates and no others. "The many," says Whitehead, "become one, and are increased by one" (*PR,* 32). The "many" refers to all of the past, to all previous actual occasions. The "one" is the new actual occasion. And for it genuinely to be new, there must be an "increase." The actual occasion is a creature. It arises from creativity, including that aspect of creativity which is formless, open, undecided, incomplete. The actual occasion makes itself from a background of completed actual occasions. These are the "many" that become "one." Obviously the "becoming" needs inspection.

1. *Becoming.* We remember that the continuum called "time" can be divided indefinitely in conception, but not in fact, for an actual occasion is a minimal unit of spatiotemporal actuality that becomes all at once (*PR,* 105-7). For purposes of dissection, however, let us pretend that it has parts which can be labeled "before" and "after" with respect to one another. And such a procedure is not mere fiction: rather it is the result of a slanted approach to an actual occasion. If we deal with the actual occasion purely on a *physical* plane, treating it as extensively given (in more familiar language, as "occupying space and time"), we find that of course the specific region of the actual occasion is divisible into subregions. "But it is only the physical pole of the actual entity which is thus divisible. The mental pole is incurably one" (*PR,* 436). If we take the actual occasion in both its physical and its mental aspects, then, only the physical lends itself to division into "before" and "after." This physical aspect is but one feature of an actual occasion, and is—as such—abstract. Whitehead writes that "physical time expresses some features of the growth, but *not* the growth of the features" (*PR,* 434; italics Whitehead's). The growth of the features requires reference to the mental pole and "how an actual occasion *becomes* constitutes *what* that actual entity is; so that the two descriptions of an actual entity are not independent" (*PR,* 34). In other words, the "coordinate" division—that in which we give spatiotemporal coordinates for an actual occasion—allows us to put as fine a microscope as we like over the constituent parts of an actual occasion conceived as merely physical. We are here in the area of sheer observation and description. Clearly, the becoming of the actual occasion must be completed in order for us to observe, describe, and (mentally) dissect it. But if we want to analyze the actual occasion as to its origins—what Whitehead calls "genetic" division (*PR,* 334-428)—we must have recourse to the mental pole of an actual occasion. Here the actual occasion can be explained only as a unit, not piecemeal. However, "in so far as the mental pole is trivial as to originality, what is inexplicable in the coordinate division (taken as actually separate) becomes thereby trivial" (*PR,* 436-37). Many "low grade" actual entities merely repeat what has, so to speak, been handed to them from nearby and nearwhen. In their case the distinction between coordinate division (into physical "parts") and genetic division (appealing to the

mental pole, the locus of possible novel origination) is unimportant, and "we are dealing with an indefinitely subdivisible extensive universe" (*PR,* 437). At this level, that of almost exclusively "physical" endurance, efficient cause is the only interesting type of cause. There is virtually no novelty—only that of temporal newness—and the ordinary meanings of the word "life," as well as the more complex in function of mentality, consciousness, imagination, and so on, simply do not apply.

In analyzing an actual occasion, so as to understand both simple examples which involve only coordinate division, and complex ones which involve high-order mental functions, we must use a blend of both coordinate division and genetic division. The procedure will thus be to lay out the genetic detail on a coordinate map. These coordinates will be both spatial, involving the idea of contemporaneity, and temporal, involving "before" and "after," "earlier" and "later," and so on.

2. *Prehensions.* The "first" level of determination, of definiteness, to which the actual entity-in-process attains, is that of prehensions. An actual occasion can be dissolved into its constituent prehensions. These prehensions are not mere qualities or characteristics. They are primarily *relations,* ways in which the actual occasion is related to previous actual occasions. Prehensions both collectively compose the actual occasion and are its relations to other actual occasions. "In the genetic-theory, the cell [the actual occasion] is exhibited as appropriating, for the foundation of its own existence, the various elements of the universe out of which it arises. Each process of appropriation of a particular element is termed a prehension" (*PR,* 335). Whitehead goes on to say that the elements appropriated are actual entities that already exist and eternal objects. Further, all actual entities are "positively prehended, but only a selection of the eternal objects."

The passage is a bit startling, since it suggests a universe in which each unit of reality comes into existence by being stuffed with all the rest. But such a specter rests on a number of easy fallacies. In the first place, an actual occasion is not "in" space and time, even if we regard it in its physical aspect alone. On the contrary, the continuously increasing network of actual occasions provides that fabric of reality whose extensive features can be considered apart from all others. These extensive features constitute the spatiotemporal continuum, the object of physical measurement. And this continuum can further be treated in its spatial aspect alone or in its temporal aspect alone. Talk of "space" and "time" is thus doubly abstract. Consequently, anything said to be "in" space or "in" time must be quite abstract. The *existence* of an actual occasion is far more concrete than these derivative features, and the specter of "stuffing" is dissolved. There is not even the risk of "stuffing" in the physical dimension alone. The "appropriation" of previous actual entities does not entail a swallowing of them, lock, stock, and barrel. It means only that there are no previous actual entities which are impertinent to (completely disconnected from) the present actual occasion, whose swift and complex biography we are investigating. For one thing, the presumption of spatial continuity and temporal continuity, necessary to all physical measurement (at least macroscopic measurement), and thus underlying all notions of physical order, requires that all actual occasions share the *same* spatiotemporal continuum. They are at least extensively connected, no matter what metric be imposed on them. Clearly, then, some selection, some choice—to use a nominally anthropomorphic word—must occur. The "choice" is not from among actual entities, but from their "contents"—the ingredient eternal objects. Entities that share a common space-time in so sharing can not wholly reject one another. Eternal objects are not, as actual entities are, primarily spatiotemporal. In themselves they are possibilities for actualization. They are not any-particular-where or any-particular-when, as actual occasions are. Strictly speaking, an actual occasion, "selecting its contents-to-be," can select from that aspect of reality which embraces the possible. The actual simply *is,* and some of it abides through any "choice." As an extreme example, consider the "life" of one physical particle in an exploding bomb. For that electron to continue to exist, there must be a series of actual occasions embodying characteristics—rather simple ones in the case of the electron—from previous actual occasions. What is repeated in the particle is a quite small "selection" of eternal objects. The existence of the electron occurs in the same continuum as does that of incarnated persons, human beings. They may be revolted or pleased by the action of the bomb—or both. And their judgments arise in the context of, and apply to, the same shared spatiotemporal world in which the electron exists. Its existence needs nothing from the realm of value judgments, however, It ignores persons *qua* persons. But men do not have this luxury. Consciousness lives more intimately and dependently with the vast realm of the physical sector than does the physical with the conscious. One price for the existence of consciousness is its dependence on the physical. This dependency often tempts us to regard the physical aspect of life as the presiding one. And it resurgently lays upon all conscious life the iron demand for social existence. No social origins, no consciousness.

So choice of a sort occurs. Some aspects of the eternal objects ingredient in previous actual occasions are seized as useful in the self-composition of an actual entity. Many are called (they are already "there"), and few are chosen. And these aspects are relational in two senses. Every eternal object is itself a doorway into the realm of eternal objects generally, every member of which is related to others. Moreover, what the actual-occasion-in-process makes of the eternal object appropriated from an existent actual occasion constitutes its relation to that actual occasion. How novel an actual occasion's use of an "appropriated" eternal object is helps to define how much "life" there is in the enduring object of which the actual occasion is a part. We shall examine this more closely in Chapter 4, but here we are concerned only with a generalized account of an actual occasion. It is in the "selection," the "choice," that the "mental" pole functions.

There is a neat contrast between the physical and mental poles. The physical pole prehends actual occasions as actual occasions in their full physicality, their extensiveness. The mental pole has for its object: eternal objects. Another way of speaking of the appearance of an actual occasion is of it as an "instance of concrescence" (PR, 321), through which a complex of prehensions become integral and concrete. A positive prehension is also termed a "feeling" (PR, 337). It is so called in order to stress the fact that while it reaches out toward existing actual entities, such reaching-out may be of a primitive sort far below the level of consciousness, intent, or perception in the ordinary senses of these terms. Whitehead underscores the not-necessarily-cognitive character of a prehension in Science and the Modern World (100-101) and says in effect that we may think of a "prehension" as an "apprehension," with the "ap-" left off, indicating that the element of consciousness may or may not be present. "Feeling" emphasizes the "subjective" side of a prehension. "Prehension" emphasizes the "grasping of the eternal" side of a feeling. Which term is to be used for these prime constituents depends on the context. But prehensions, we must remember, are either negative or positive, either rejecting the contents of available actual occasions or some part of them as nonuseful, or appropriating elements from them. Feelings are always positive, although selective.

3. *The Integration of Feelings.* A feeling, a positive prehension, can be understood in terms of (1) "subject," that is, the actual-entity-in-process; (2) the out-there, the data which are available; (3) the ignored or rejected data, the negative features of selection; (4) the "objective datum," positively felt; and (5) the "subjective form," which is the mode or way in which the data are felt.[1]

(1) We are here considering an incomplete subject, the actual occasion in process. Whitehead calls it a "microprocess," as opposed to the "macroprocess." The latter is process conceived in terms of the continuity of the creativity embodied in its enduring creatures. But here we fasten our attention on a single cell, a single actual occasion and what is going on "inside it." The single actual occasion comes into being and perishes in a minimum unit of time. *It does not endure.* Only temporally linked-together clusters (nexūs) of actual occasions collectively comprise "enduring objects." The single actual occasion perishes and becomes "immortal," that is, fixed in an invariant past.

(2) The out-there (my term) is the already accomplished, and thereby immortalized world. This world is complete only insofar as we consider it as objective and as accessible for use by the oncoming actual occasion. But the world is incomplete by reason of the surge of creativity that permeates it. This surge is exemplified in the advance of temporality, with its newly emerging creatures.

(3) All the "world" is there, but not all of it can be used. Each actual occasion represents a complex selection and rejection of what the world has to offer. Much of the world will share with the new actual occasion only the very general character of concrescence, which requires the same spatiotemporal continuum for all actual occasions. Small wonder that when we find a temporally extended chain of actual occasions, each of which varies but little from its predecessors, so that the mental pole is not very active, and the ensuing novelty is slight, we dub the enduring object exhibiting such invariant continuity, a *physical*

object. And, accordingly, we seize upon its measure-properties as its final reality. Some vague intuition of this sort surely underlies Locke's ill-fated discernment of "primary" qualities.

(4) The "objective datum" is the name for any entity which has something to offer in the way of a useful constituent to the actual occasion in its process of self-making through the integration of feelings.

(5) The "subjective form" is the use to which the actual occasion in process puts the positively prehended datum. This subjective form is best seen simply in Whitehead's remark: "No two occasions can have identical worlds" *(PR,* 321). There is, he means, an incurable privacy of perspective in any actual occasion. This privacy of perspective is thus an ineradicable feature of the concrete world, for that world is composed of actual occasions. But this plunges us into no Cartesian abyss, no dualism of mind and body without a bridge. For such privacy of perspective requires a public object to be private about. However, "no element in the universe [is] capable of pure privacy" *(PR,* 324).

The confluence of subjective elements and objective elements in the complex actual occasions that are present in human consciousness is quite commonplace. The housekeeper grimly reaches for the spray-gun, and the baby daughter reaches blindly; but if the householder is an arachnidologist, he may restrain the impulse to kill for the sake of investigating the common object of the three attentions: a spider. The reactions betray the differences of perspective. But to treat the datum agreed upon—"spider"—as real and the reaction or valuation, as Whitehead would call it, as somehow part of an unreal world or as part of another order of reality, separate and distinct from the agreed-upon one, can only be regarded as arbitrary. The fear, the curiosity, and the articulated interest are as "real" as the spider. Indeed either the spider or the evaluation laid upon it can be considered separately only by an act of abstraction. And then we are no longer at the level of the actual, the concrete.

"Subjective form" immediately introduces the topic of valuation which branches into two considerations: the degree to which "consciousness" is present in evaluation, and the analysis of eternal objects, which are possible values for an actual occasion.

The selection of data then is really a two-phase occurrence: *what* and *how*. Whitehead says, "All the actual entities are positively prehended [felt], but only a selection of the eternal objects" (*PR*, 335). And the selected eternal object is capable of a variety of significant uses in any given actual occasion. *How* an actual occasion becomes constitutes what sort of entity it is, and depends upon what use it makes of the eternal objects it prehends. The feelings, according to Whitehead, "are inseparable from the end at which they aim; and this end is the feeler. The feelings aim at the feeler, as their final cause" (*PR*, 339).

In the modalities of *how* the objective data are employed and exploited lies the question of the presence of consciousness. This topic will be investigated in Chapters 5 to 7. As a holding action we may quote and expand one citation from Whitehead: "Consciousness arises when a synthetic feeling integrates physical and conceptual feelings" (*PR*, 371). A "physical feeling" of an actual occasion for antecedent ones is one in which the already existing feeling is felt *qua* actual occasion. A "conceptual" feeling is a feeling whose datum is an eternal object. The primary case of such a conceptual feeling is thus one in which the actual-entity-in-process takes account of an ingredient eternal object as eternal object. There is interconnectedness of elements in the realm of eternal objects, and there is also a vast multiplicity of possible ways in which these eternal objects may ingress. Thus the conceptual feeling, arising in the mental pole, and dealing primarily with eternal objects—pure possibles—stretches the actual occasion's grasp, from the *given* actual eternal object, into what might have been or might be, but *is* not. The conceptual feeling is thus the foundation of all imagination, consciousness, and *ordered* novelty. It does not matter which green autumn leaf reminds me of the clear Mediterranean on a July morning; my reaction of nostalgia and the sudden ingress of a thousand memories come rushing—almost "by themselves." The same green leaf, on that tree, here and now, may be just the evidence the gardener wants that the plant is healthy. He is involved in no free flight of imagination. The where and when of the green, (the spatiotemporality) is the first and basic feeling he must have, before he can in his way and his mode, advance to the conceptual realm of significance. But the conjugation of the present with the past, or with the future, in the mode of personal appreciation and esthetic delight, or in the mode of practical action, all represent a transcendence of the here and now. Such transcendence of the actual is an exploration of what has been or might have been or must be or could not be or might be—or more likely, some combination of these. This exploration is grounded firmly in the nonactual, but nonetheless real, the realm of eternal objects. It is this that Whitehead has in mind when he says, "The future is merely real, without being actual; whereas the past is a nexus of actualities" [from which, as such, all "possibility" has evaporated] (*PR*, 327).

The above five aspects of the act of feeling, through which an actual occasion creates itself, can be looked at from a different and somewhat less detailed side. Beginning with the actual occasion considered as a completed harmony (that is, an integration) of feelings, we can see the occasion as the outcome of a threefold process (*PR*, 32).

(1) A phase of relative passivity. This is the phase in which the occasion-to-be is just born, nascent, open. Whitehead calls it the "responsive" phase, and he elsewhere underscores the passivity by speaking of the actual world so given to the young actual occasion as the "causal part" of that occasion. The phrase is tricky, since the basic form of causation is the self-causation of the actual occasion from the background of the actual world.[2] But Whitehead immediately makes it clear that there is no "the" actual world, but always an actual world *for some* actual occasion, with disparities between such actual worlds dependent upon the actual occasions in question (*PR*, 256). This is the difference of "perspective" mentioned above. Thus even in the "responsive phase" there is no sheer passivity, the idiosyncrasy of an actual occasion being evident from the first.

(2) The "supplemental" stage. This is where the action is. Since the human consciousness, which immediate intuition gives us, has its roots in this phase, and since there is relatively little exploitation of this phase by mere primitive occasions, Whitehead uses warmly biomorphic and anthropomorphic language in describing this phase. It may be broken into subphases, an esthetic subphase and an intellectual subphase. The "esthetic" subphase derives its name from the Greek word for *sense*. This is sense conceived as the generic tendency of any living being to encounter the world evaluatively, if only at the level of "aversion" and "adversion." This is the level at which we often decide whether or not some enduring object is "alive," in the familiar sense of

"living." Where it shows some sign of preference for or against, we suspect it of an internality, of some privacy of perspective, not directly observable, but behaviorly inferrable. The most rudimentarily preferential act would be a summary chain of actual occasions sharing an abiding theme of purpose: the blind invasion of a cell by a virus, for instance. This is not an intellective, conscious, or reflective purpose. It can be quite predictable. It may be the sheerest "physical" purpose (v. *PR,* 280), but it is not simple mechanical response. Simple physical feelings may be called "causal" feelings (e.g., *PR,* 361), but their adjustment to one another in the supplemental phase is not a sheer confluence. This is the level at which we find the roots of emotion, the one at which (using language normally reserved for life of a relatively complex sort) "perception is heightened by its assumption of pain and pleasure, beauty and distaste" *(PR,* 325). The other subphase of this second stage is dubbed "intellectual." If this phase be wanting or slight, then the adventure into the realm of eternal objects as pure potentials is accordingly feeble. To that extent the actual occasion is "blind." It adjusts esthetically the available data, treats them de facto, and expends its originality on selective assimilation. But wherever the contrast between an eternal object as a given ingredient in an actual occasion and other eternal objects, not given but relevant, occurs, the intellectual subphase is active. Clearly it is itself supplementary to the esthetic phase, and—following our procedure of spreading out the genetic division of actual occasions on a coordinate map—it must be said to be "later."

(3) Finally there is the "satisfaction." This term also must be resolved first into its etymology. "Satis-facere" is to "make enough," to "manufacture" a "satiety." It is the closing up of the actual entity. This is "the culmination marking the evaporation of all determination . . . . But the process itself lies in the two former phases" *(PR,* 323). The satisfaction is the beginning of the end, the present edge of what will shortly be past, immortal. It is a *decision*—speaking etymologically, a *cutting-off.* The aftermath of this decision is, like the coming-to-be of the actual occasion itself, a dual affair. It is microscopically complete; that is, its external process is satisfied, and no further internal changes are possible. But its external fortunes—what the oncoming future will make of it—are still incomplete. It has passed from subject to

"super-ject" and thereby takes up a status as object (*PR*, 134-36). This is the meaning of an early and opaque remark of Whitehead's in *Process and Reality:* "The concrescence of each individual actual entity is internally determined and is externally free" (p. 41).

CHAPTER 4

Life, and the Organization of Actual Occasions

I *Life and Emergent Novelty*

Aristotle lays out, in his clean taxonomic way, four major types of alterable beings: material, inanimate things; plants; animals; and men. There seems little doubt that the distinctions are present in Plato, who had less affection for final categorization than did Aristotle. But both philosophers, thinking of temporality as cyclic—embodied in the recurrence of seasons, astral positions, and so on—had no need of asking themselves about borderline cases. A forebear of Aristotle, Empedocles, had a curious heuristic myth of natural selection without a doctrine of evolution. And Aristotle seems to have been near to some faint supposition of evolution *within* the human kind. For example, he regarded certain rational beings—barbarians—as rational insofar as they can respond to reason, but not insofar as they cannot reason for their own welfare. These "natural slaves," as the unfortunate translation usually runs, are nonetheless human. Moreover, he was aware of the evolution of social men, whose insights are embodied in better or less able constitutions and types of government. Since men are as essentially social (*"zoon politikon"* strictly means "polis-dwelling animal") as they are rational, they clearly may be regarded as gradient in their rationality, for rationality and sociality mutually require one another. But if this be evolution, or the preparation for it, it is a mild form; and the idea of a gradient condition between men and animals is wanting in classical thought.

The advent of the Christian doctrine of linear time, once secularized and separated from the Judaeo-Christian presentations of creation, set the stage for the Darwinian hypothesis. This hypothesis has almost invariably been construed as requiring the graded emergence of more complex organisms from simpler ones, with some devolutionary countercurrents. There is some recent speculation, too partial to assess, that the rate of evolution has changed radically from time to time, but the conception of genuine discontinuity has never seriously held the stage. Chickens produce eggs and vice versa, with minor changes which cumulatively cohere to become major changes. There are questions surrounding this notion, but Whitehead does not raise them. He takes the graduated hypothesis as a background assumption and sets about constructing a vocabulary and concepts which will accommodate to this hypothesis. In so doing he passes well beyond the more cautious boundaries of standard biological doctrine. As has been suggested, he sometimes speaks of "life" as if it were a universal category, present in some degree in all actuality. At other times, he recognizes the acute practicality of limiting the word "life" to what exhibits ordered and internal change, through appropriation of external elements. By and large, Whitehead's notion is that life is a matter of degree. We recall that he says of life that it is a "bid for freedom." And such freedom is always tangibly embodied in novelty, incorporated into the order of the living being.

It is interesting to notice that common usage supports this view. We speak of a man as "lively" when his responses to his immediate environment are quick, adaptive, fresh. "What sort of a guy is Professor Filboid?" "Dead." The answer is summary and hardly requires elaboration.

Speaking a little more technically, the actual occasions that constitute an enduring object exhibit life in proportion as they do not merely conform. All actual occasions have a mental pole, and Whitehead, in *Process and Reality,* clings to this technical notion. But elsewhere he yields a bit to popular usage to make a point:

> In its lowest form, mental experience is canalized into slavish conformity. . . . [which] pervades all nature. It is rather a capacity for mentality, than mentality itself. But it *is* mentality. . . . it produces no disturbance of the repetitive character of physical fact. . . . It is degraded to being merely one of the actors in the efficient causation.
>
> But when mentality is working at a high level, it brings novelty into, the appetitions of mental experience. (*FR*, 27)

Even here Whitehead does not abandon his notion that "the root principles of life are, in some lowly form, exemplified in all types of physical existence" (*FR*,17).

II *The Organization of Actual Occasions*

Strictly speaking, "no single occasion can be called living. Life is the coördination of the mental spontaneities throughout the occasions of a society" (*AI*, 266). This theme leads us to ask immediately about the ways in which groups of actual occasions can be organized. Nor should we be deterred too much by an apparent contradiction to the above remark: "Thus a single occasion is alive when the subjective aim which determines its process of concrescence has introduced a novelty of definiteness not to be found in the inherited data of its primary phase" (*PR*, 159). The two remarks can be put together in the following way: Consider any single actual occasion by itself and you have nothing to identify as alive. It is alive only to the extent that it bears certain relationships of conformity to previous and intimately related actual occasions together with certain "mental spontaneities" ("novelty of definiteness" in the second quotation) arising from itself alone. An organism—that is, a particularly organized group of actual occasions—is said to be "alive," when "in some measure its reactions are inexplicable by *any* tradition of pure physical inheritance" (*ibid.*).

Everything, then, turns on the way in which actual occasions are grouped, and the types of order to be found in these groupings.

The most general term for a group of actual occasions is a "nexūs." And the simplest kind of nexus is one in which there is no temporal connectivity. The flash of color on suddenly lit water, or of an explosion against the sky, or the briefest whiff of smell, enough to be objectified for some subject, is such a nexus. It may be bound to other nexūs and they enclosed within still more complex ones, for there are nexūs of nexūs of nexūs in increasing complexity. But in itself it is the simplest case of a group, one which is, so to speak, only one actual occasion thick along a time line. Its extent is purely spatial. All nexūs must exhibit some principle of order, if only to be distinguished from a mere heap or collection of actual occasions. This simple nexūs has no history *within* itself, however. The "mutual immanence," which means the internal relatedness of the members of the nexus, is given in their sharing a common quality or set of qualities in a common space.

All other nexūs are "societies" of one kind or another, and exhibit temporal order, with or without spatial order. The members of a temporally ordered nexūs are at least some of them conjoined according to the relationship of before and after. Therefore such nexūs indicate internal components of causal connection. Another way of stating this internal causal order, which is a prime feature of societies, is to say that they exhibit among themselves "reproduction" of prehensions (*AI*, 261). In short, a society is an *enduring* nexus. To say that these actual occasions are internally related is not to give more than the general relationship which holds among all actual entities. All are internally related. Since each has made itself from the stockpile of the rest, it is clear that any particular actuality is *ipso facto* internally related to the past actual occasions in just the sense that Whitehead intends: to be internally related to something else, a thing must be what it is by reason of what something else is. We come here to an essential feature of Whitehead's rejection of a substance metaphysics. A chair is what it is, as a separable substance, regardless of most of what is around it, or where it is. Such disconnection of the chair, or any substance, is just what disqualifies it from being a fundamental unit of reality. The general classic definition of a substance as that which "exists in and through itself" should warn us that we are dealing with abstractions, not basics. Over against substantial objects externally (nonessentially) related to one another, Whitehead poses actual occasions, minimal events, time-structured and internally (essentially) related to one another.

Excursus on the problem of mutual immanence. What is harder to understand in Whitehead is the *mutual* immanence of actual occasions belonging to the same society. That the most recent actual occasions should be essentially what they are by their more or less novel adaptation of elements given from past members of the society is not too difficult to see. But *mutual* immanence further requires that the past actualities be internally related to present ones. The idea of internal relations does not necessarily entail that, given two *relata, A* and *B*, if *A* is internally related to *B*, then *B* is internally related to *A*. For example, Whitehead specifically asserts that eternal objects are *externally* related to actual entities. That is, whatever actual entities there may be does not alter the "individual essence" of an eternal object. But what eternal objects there are sharply limits and thus helps to define the actual occasion. The occasion depends for its being on eternal objects, but they, as mere possibles, do not depend for what they "are" on particular actual occasions. (See *SMW*, Chapter 10, passim, e.g., pp. 229-30.)

Since "immanence" or "internal relatedness" is not necessarily a reciprocal relation, it follows that the mutual immanence of actual occasions must be assignable to some activity within the organism. The difficulty is that any completed actual occasion has lost all internal activity. As finished, its moment of creativity has come and gone. It abides in the past, but its activity has ceased. If P be a past event and N a present one forming now in the same society, then P and N are mutually immanent. This entails that N is determinative of what P is. But P is over and finished. What has N to offer P, then? The answer is that P's being closed up means the cessation of all becoming internally. But P can play many roles in many actual occasions to come—in fact, an indefinite number. These actual occasions adapt elements from P, each occasion doing this in its own perspective. P's internal biography may be at an end, but its status and role in the future are still open, still incomplete. We recall that Whitehead says of each actual occasion that it is "internally determined and externally free." We have been considering one interpretation of this phrase.

Yet a problem remains. It is at least a problem of terminology. "Mutual immanence" means "mutually internally related." P is said to be externally free for subsequent now-times and now-occasions, N_1, N_2, N_3, etc. Yet its relations with any actual occasion are supposed to be internal. Whitehead is not unaware of the problem. He says, "Thus each actual entity, although complete so far as concerns its microscopic process, is yet incomplete by reason of its objective inclusion of the macroscopic process. It really experiences a future which must [come to] be actual . . ." (*PR*, 327-28). This hardly solves the problem, although it clarifies it a bit, for we still seem to be confronted with an ambiguity in the meaning of "external-internal."

Neither is the problem trivial nor dominantly verbal, since on the relation between present and past rest two primary questions: those of the determinism of the present and the alterability of the past. Our task, however, is primarily exegesis, and we continue with the levels of societies of actual occasions, leaving a question mark over the subject of "mutual immanence."

III *Primates*

In *Science and the Modern World* Whitehead deals with what he calls *primates.* These may be thought of as the simplest enduring organisms. They would be only one actual occasion "wide" (in space) but composed of many actual occasions temporally, each one replacing the last. If we think of a single actual occasion as being serially replaced, with changes only in spatial and temporal coordinates, and confine ourselves to the organism's physical aspect alone (which is about all it would have), we have a primate. There would then be simple qualitative identity passed along from actual occasion to actual occasion, with possible changes as to spatiotemporal measurement (depending on whether or not the particle is in motion). Such characteristics as mass and charge would presumably qualify, for Whitehead is trying to stipulate what the ideally simple physical particle would look like, in the philosophy of organism.

Have we such primates? Alternatively, have we any candidates? Our best laboratory-determined candidates are protons and electrons (*SMW*, 191; cf. p. 194, however), but Whitehead—perhaps remembering the ill-starred naming of the "atom"—only tentatively accepts these candidates, since their nature is contingent on laboratory experiment. But, as he says, "the aspects of a primate are merely its contributions to the electro-magnetic field. This is in fact exactly what we know of electrons and protons" (*ibid.*).

In his mature philosophy Whitehead never recurs to the subject of primates. It was developed merely to show how a troublesome problem in the quantum theory of the time (1924) could not only be understood in terms of a philosophy of organism, but would actually contribute something to such a philosophy. Briefly, the problem is this: certain experiments in microphysics seemed to require that an electron suffers temporal discontinuity. The electron, if visualized, seemed to be nowhere at all, in the continuum, during certain critical phases of its career. Yet the waves associated with its existence have to be thought of as propagated continuously, without gaps. How come? Whitehead's answer can only be stated in caricature here.[1] The waves associated with, say, an electron's existence cluster together in some stretches of time in such a way as to constitute stable material configurations. At other times, they tend to cancel one another, and nothing like material existence is present. Two physicists at about the same time (Schrödinger and De Broglie) developed similar "wave-packet" metaphors for the electron. The theory also allows for the dissolving of the average energy of a particle into sheer radiation, diffusion of free electromagnetic waves.

The success or failure of the theory of primates would only be a distraction here, especially since subsequent developments in physics seem to require that we leave off making "pictures" of ultimate physical particles at all. But it serves as a useful beginning point for ascending the scale of complexity of societies of actual occasions. For the primate may be considered as the result of a harmless abstraction from the simplest kind of society having temporal order and no spatial extent other than that of a single occasion. The primate is evidently such a society, with its "mental side" ignored. But the leaving out of the mental side is hardly objectionable if the mentality of each actual occasion is expended in a mere repetition of what qualitatively happened before.

The primate evidently does exhibit a kind of order that is of prime importance in the study of more complex organisms, however. This is "personal order."

IV *Personal Order*

Whitehead defines personal order without immediately appealing to the idea of time. A nonrigorous summary of this definition (*PR*, 50-51) is as follows: personal order belongs to a society when its members (actual occasions) are organized serially. "Serially" means that, except for the first and last members of the society, any member of the society either "inherits" from, or is inherited from by, every other member of the society, adjacent or not. What is "inherited" must clearly be of central importance, representing either the only identity among the various members, or the dominant identity. The result is that, as an example of the "only identity" case, we have the electron as an enduring object. In the case of a "dominant identity," we have a man (*PR,* 141; *AI,* 263-265). The term "personal" therefore does not refer necessarily to anything conscious or even living, as ordinarily understood. On the other hand, "The only strictly personal society of which we have direct discriminative intuition is the society of our own personal experiences" (*AI,* 265). In order to bring a "living human person" into focus, the mere technical definition of a *person* will not take us very far. We must probe the organization of societies a bit further.

V   *Living Societies*

In both *Process and Reality* and *Adventures of Ideas* Whitehead uses the word "living" very broadly. At times, he seems to want the word "living" to apply in some measure to any actuality. At other times, he seems to want to keep the word for more restricted uses. We have already seen that it is probably best to regard "living" and "non-living" as matters of degree. The degree to which there is an introduction and incorporation of novelty is the degree to which life is present (e.g., *AI,* 266 and *PR,* 156). Though Whitehead occasionally speaks of "living occasions," it is best to think of life as a feature of a society of occasions. Novelty is, after all, novelty in respect of something else (*ibid.*; also *PR,* 158). The incorporation of novelty means that the novelty is not merely disruptive, but rather that there is the maintenance of, or increase in, an order of complexity.

Not only must there be some incarnated novelty in a series of actual occasions, in order for there to be life, but there also must be an assimilation of food. This means that there must be a disintegration of a complex neighboring society into simpler components suitable for assimilation. Bluntly, "life is robbery. It is at this point that with life morals become acute. The robber requires justification" (*PR,* 160). A discussion of the order of nature is primarily an account of and an emphasis upon the de facto features of nature. It is worth remarking of this observation of Whitehead's—itself a passing remark—that the language of "robbery" and "justification" are deliberately anthropomorphic; they point the reader's attention to a human situation. If you wish to develop a moral theory—a thing Whitehead did not do—then you may begin with the material obligation which any living thing owes to its material environment. This material obligation (not Whitehead's term) is coordinate with the material doctrine of immortality mentioned at the end of Chapter 2. Any doctrine of spirit (as to immortality) or of obligation (as to morality) which proposes to isolate itself from material fact is as surely guilty of "misplaced concreteness" as is materialism itself. Normally, when Whitehead speaks of "misplaced concreteness" he has in mind the tendency we have to think of what is material as being fundamental, concrete. This distillation of the physical from the mental is a confusion of an abstraction (matter) with the actual (actual occasions) from which it has been abstracted. But any substituting of either the purely physical or the purely mental aspects of actuality for that actuality itself is an example of the "Fallacy of Misplaced Concreteness" (*SMW,* 84-85).[2] It is not just materialists who make this blunder. Whitehead's theme, indirectly indicated here, is that one can be equally abstract about the nonmaterial aspects of actuality.

These two indices of "living societies"—the degree of novelty and the assimilation and exploitation of the environment—are the groundwork for a third characteristic of a living society: a living society is built upon inorganic ones. For example, salt is salt, be it in my body or in the sea. There are complex "organic" (the chemist's meaning of "organic" overlaps with Whitehead's here, but not completely) societies that do not normally occur, save in the living society as a whole. Even hearts have been kept functioning in isolation, out of bodies, by a duplication of bodily conditions, but under the guidance and control of other living persons.[3] A "living society" always will have some strands in its hierarchy of nexūs that have genuinely original reactions, others that are largely nonoriginal. Within or without my body, salt and water are salt and water. The originative nexūs which are, metaphorically, perched atop the substrate of nonliving nexūs require the latter in order to exist. "We do not know of any living society devoid of its subservient apparatus of inorganic societies," says Whitehead (*PR,* 157). The originative nexūs he calls "entirely living," since they encompass the significant (sources of our) novel origination, but cannot strictly be called a society, evidently by reason of their insufficiency for independent survival.

VI   *Living Persons*

A living person is the confluence of personal order and an entirely living nexus with its subordinate mechanism of nonliving, inorganic nexūs. The personal order is present when there is a central strand of a quite integral nature which embodies a profound and central continuity. The livingness of something depends upon the degree of integral novelty generated and maintained within the total order. In a sense, the identity of a personal order is at odds with the introduced novelty which characterizes life. "It is not of the essence of life to be a living person. Indeed a living person requires that its immediate environment be a living, non-social nexus" (*PR*, 163). By "immediate environment" Whitehead means the inorganic substratum of a body to which its organic parts can be reduced. There is, therefore, "no necessary connection" between "life" and "personality" (*AI*, 266). All the same, our own self-awareness in personal experience is of such personality and is, as we have seen, the only unmediated encounter which we have with personality (*PR*, 164 and *AI*, 265).

Whitehead's doctrine of "personal life" is thus of a very tenuous semi-entity. Personality demands continuity, but life demands novelty. It follows that life defined as "the teleological introduction of novelty, with some conformation of objectives" (*AI*, 266) must be subtly analyzed in that particular aspect which is called "personal life." Whitehead's view here clearly conforms to the well-known problems in the legal conception of personal responsibility. When, for example, the law finds a minor unprosecutable by the same rules as those that apply to adults, it presumably is arguing that the thread of personal order (and therefore responsibility) is not yet sufficiently formed. Again with adults the degree of premeditation which justifies the severest penalties is an index of the settled continuity of the person prosecuted. A man who murders in understandable rage, overwhelmed by what is before him, is generally judged more leniently and is sometimes wholly exonerated. The leniency is a warrant of the fragility of personality and therefore of responsibility. In general, we say of a man, "He is not himself," or, more sentimentally, "That's not the *real* Jack."

With this outline of Whitehead's analysis of the living order there arise two other themes. Whitehead's treatment of the living person branches in two directions. The personal living society "is the man defined as a person [rather than as the total complex of largely material elements]. It is the soul of which Plato spoke" (*AI*, 267). But also, "The defining characteristic of a living person is some definite type of hybrid prehensions transmitted from occasion to occasion of its existence" (*PR*, 163). Hybrid prehensions lead us into Whitehead's theory of perception; the doctrine of the soul leads us to Whitehead's view of the divine nature. These themes require separate—though necessarily not independent—treatment. We turn first to the theory of hybrid prehensions, which applies in the context of the theory of consciousness.

CHAPTER 5

Body and Mind (A): Perception

I *The Mind-Body Problem*

Beginning with his early writings in the philosophy of science, Whitehead was concerned with the disastrous split between mind and nature that had plagued both the British empiricists—Locke, Berkeley, Hume—and the continental rationalists from Descartes to Kant. Mental operations and physical things being superficially so distinct from one another, philosophers had treated them in such a way as to raise the question not only of how they *are* related, but of how they possibly *could* be related. In general, three kinds of answer had been given: that mentality be subsumed under materiality, that materiality be dissolved into mentality, and that the two coexist with tenuous connections between them, the latter to be determined by investigation and/or reflection. Subtle variations on these themes, coupled with an inconsistent awareness that the answers were vulnerable, all but constitute the history of major philosophical thought between Descartes and Kant. After the fatigue of these centuries, the principal advances in the problem of the relation between body and mind sometimes seemed to be in agreement on the fallacies to be discarded. But even here unanimity is hard to find.

Spinoza alone glimpsed some transcendence of the problem. In this matter many philosophers would argue that he excelled the man who is, in so many ways, his superior: Immanuel Kant. Spinoza insisted that mentality and physicality were but different aspects of the same reality. This reality, many-faceted, indeed infinitely faceted, turns but two of its aspects, physical and mental, toward man, who is part of the same reality. Spinoza is himself hardly unassailable, but—like Whithead—he was a mathematician. He constructed his philosophy deliberately along the lines of a systematic geometry. His model was Euclid. And, like Whitehead to follow nearly three centuries later, he knew that deductive persuasiveness (with its self-demand of internal consistency) depends on making the basic convictions of systematic thought believable in their formulation and far-ranging in their consequences. Early in his masterpiece, *The Ethics,* Spinoza develops the notion of the double aspect of reality and shortly undertakes to show how and why some things appear more in one light and others in another.

Whitehead takes a similar posture, differing from Spinoza basically in the same way that William James does, namely by holding a pluralistic view of the universe, composed of *many* real entities, with the reality of time and the openness of the future as basic assumptions. Spinoza's view is monistic and deterministic, there being but one primary and total reality which is nature or God—they are the same—changeless and perfect, and inclusive of all apparently individual things. This astonishing notion is remarkably defensible, but explanation of it is out of place here. However, no defense would have deterred William James from espousing immediate experience as directly revealing the real. In this Whitehead follows James, acknowledging his indebtedness to both James and Spinoza. Moreover, James's refusal to regard time as illusory develops, in Whitehead, into the full-fledged doctrine of creativity which that refusal implies.

James occupied himself primarily with human experience. Whitehead's task is larger: a comprehensive metaphysics that can accommodate the needs and hypotheses of physical science as well as those of direct human experience. It is in this framework that we must approach Whitehead's doctrine of consciousness.

The foundation of Whitehead's views can be summarized as follows: From his days as a philosopher of science he keeps the conviction that science investigates and penetrates reality as surely as does ordinary experience. From James he draws the assumption that the way to get at the mind-body problem is by accepting their mutual relatedness as the beginning point to be analyzed, not defined out of existence. And from evolutionary doctrine, as we have seen, he inherits the conviction that the scale of reality, from simplest entities to man, is a standing picture of the way the world has developed.

Accordingly, Whitehead's basic unit, the actual occasion, is treated as fundamentally bipolar. We must now trace the organization of actual occasions from the internal functioning of a single complex actual occasion to the interoccasional functions of a temporal series of actual occasions. It is only in such a series that there can be any activity—even nonconscious—of the sort that we would normally call "mental."

II *Hybrid Prehensions*

All actual occasions have a mental pole. This mental pole gives rise to or is embodied in the actual occasion's conceptual prehensions, which deal with eternal objects as such. Physical prehensions, pure physical prehensions, are concerned only with the *is,* the actual. But the conceptual prehension is the doorway to the *might be,* the possible. Thus the roots of imagination lie deep in the order of the actual, but are not confined to it. Since imagination deals with the possible, it arises from the mental poles of actual occasions, manifesting itself in the most primitive condition of life: appetition, which is the struggle from the background of what *is* toward what *is not,* but could be. (See, e.g., *PR,* 48-49.)

It is thus the essence of mentality that no actual occasion deals merely with the given as given. Even in the most blind and automatic repetition, the mental pole is functioning, it seizes its eternal object(s) in at least partial divorce from the(ir) given ingression. It is the interconnectedness among eternal objects that opens the possibility of novelty for the mental pole. But the novelty is not mere free exploration of the realm of the possible by way of this entry to eternal objects generally. The process of origination is more complex. It involves a third kind of prehension, a derivative one, the "hybrid prehension."

Hybrid prehensions are considered only slightly even in some quite technical discussions of Whitehead's philosophy, though they are at the very foundation of his treatment of the relation between mind and body. Commentators tend to spare the reader examples, largely confining themselves to close and analytic paraphrase of Whitehead's remarks. We shall hope to avoid popular clarifications of the run-Jane-run variety, as well as the fine-grained expositions that are the standard playing boards of experts. Discussion of hybrid prehensions must risk the latter extreme, however, in the interests of a general grasp of Whitehead's philosophy.

Whitehead lays great stress on hybrid prehensions: "Consciousness arises when a synthetic feeling integrates physical and conceptual feelings" (*PR,* 371). And earlier: "It is impossible to scrutinize too carefully the character to be assigned to the datum in the act of experience. The whole philosophical system depends on it" (*PR,* 238).

The datum is whatever is given to an actual occasion for its use in its act of self-comprising; how it handles the datum defines how the actual occasion becomes and therefore what it is. The fundamental base line for all transmission is physical. The physical is the *sine qua non.* But it is equally true that there is nothing which is both purely physical and concrete. The "Category of Conceptual Valuation" states a general rule: that from every physical feeling there arises a "purely conceptual feeling" which has as its datum *not* the precedent actual occasion(s) but the eternal object(s) ingredient in the occasion (*PR,* 39-40). This conceptual feeling is an essential ingredient in any actual occasion or nexus of actual occasions (some eternal objects—colors, for example—seem to require nexūs for embodiment, rather than single actual occasions). When such a conceptual feeling in one actual occasion becomes itself the datum for another conceptual feeling, without physical reinforcement (or at least independently of such physical reinforcement), we have what Whitehead calls a "hybrid physical prehension," or more briefly, "a hybrid prehension." "Thus a pure physical prehension is the transmission of physical feeling, while hybrid prehension is the transmission of mental feeling" (*PR,* 469). Mentality may necessarily require physical undergirding in order to occur. We know of no case where it does not. But what constitutes the object of interest for an actual occasion, and therefore what functions as a dominant factor in its self-composition, may be a conceptual feeling with its referent eternal object. Whitehead is wisely distinguishing between the *means* of mental functioning, which as a process is not isolable from its physical aspect, and the *materials* for such functioning, through which the actual occasion receives its major determinations. He thus avoids one of the commonest stupidities in the history of the mind-body problem: the assumption that because no mentality occurs without physicality, the former must on principle be reducible to the latter.

Paradoxically, the easiest analogies are the most complicated ones—those that come in our own conscious experience—simply because of the privileged view which we have of it. Consider the following analogy: Suppose an artist, in one glance, to estimate his work-in-progress. He will see it in many ways, a set of mere pigments, a representation of a model before him, the embodiment of his feelings, perhaps the cause of his fatigue, and so on. This inspection, with its multiple aspects and its almost innumerable possible consequences, may also embody an uneasiness. Something is wrong. The "satisfaction" of his glance is an act charged with emotional and intellective significance; but the "satisfaction" is merely a completion of the act of inspection, "satisfaction" in Whitehead's technical sense. The artist, with his antecedent aims, vaguely still felt, and his open future before him, is not satisfied in the popular sense of the word. Now it is the "still felt" that we must concentrate upon. Something has been passed along, conceptually. The concept itself constitutes a thread of order along a series of actual occasions, binding them together as features of an enduring object—the artist in his full physicality. The mutating enduring object—the painting—is itself only partly understandable in terms of its physical components and indeed their physical model (I confine myself here to a representational work of art). It represents an accumulated order surviving the concrete acts that have serially given rise to its component parts: brush stroke upon brush stroke. The—thus far incomplete—order itself is a faint mirror of the surviving intent of the artist.

But now something is wrong. The intent is not emerging in fact. Let us give the story a happy ending. The artist sees a flat shadow that is done too much in gray and black. He wants a warmer, more vital contrast. He mixes the complementary color on his palette, for skin-pink a dusty green, paints over the old gray and suddenly the skin looks alive, vibrant; something of life has been caught and held.

For illustrative purposes the example will do; for analytic purposes, it is unduly complex. But it serves to make two Whiteheadian points: (1) That every ingression of an eternal object has some emotive tone.

This is oblique to our present interest; we must put it aside. (2) That every conceptual feeling is an act of negation.

We must, then, further concentrate on the negation. In the example above the negation lies in the discrepancy between emotive intent passed along from unit of consciousness to unit of consciousness, and the nagging failure of the growing painting to satisfy the intent. There is an aim, and the aim is toward something *not* given, *not* there already. Conceivably it may have even cost the artist a considerable series of reflections to specify that it is the color which is off. But the basic "not this," "not that" acts lie much deeper, not as disturbing factors, but as the sheer discriminative process underlying all judgment. Every conceptual entertainment has as its object the discriminated eternal object, regardless of how acquired. *The primary act of negation, the tap root of all negations, is the recognition of the ingredient object as different from the actual occasion in which it ingresses.* Whitehead puts it this way: "Conceptual feeling is the feeling of unqualified negation; that is to say, it is the feeling of a definite eternal object with the definite extrusion of any particular realization" (*PR,* 372). Such conceptual feeling is not to be regarded as a segment of consciousness, or even awareness; "all awareness, even awareness of concepts, requires at least the synthesis of physical feelings with conceptual feeling" (*ibid.*). Whitehead precedes his analysis of consciousness as arising through the synthesis of physical and conceptual feelings with the remark that "a pure concept does not involve consciousness, at least in our human experience" (*PR,* 371). Furthermore, "affirmation involves its contrast with negation, and negation involves its contrast with affirmation. . . . Consciousness is how we feel the affirmation-negation contrast" (*PR,* 372).

So we have well overshot our mark if the uneasy painter is regarded primarily as an example of the basic negation, rather than as an analogy. He is conscious, his act is cumulative, his negativity is a feature of a vast nexus of actual occasions, his aim survives through such occasions, and the adjustment of his aim does also. What has been illustrated, in spite of the foregoing defects, is that every act is synthesized around an aim, deals with materials independent of their mode of origination, is selective and discriminative in its synthesis, and is disciplined by both physical fact and relevant concepts. It is this last feature that we pursue further in the single actual occasion. The word "relevant" is promissory. Let us unpack it to see what it contains.

The fact that each physical feeling by an actual occasion of another actual occasion "registers" as a conceptual feeling lies under both the dualism of fact and value and that of mind and body. Fact and value are discussed in Chapters 8 and 9 but are briefly pertinent here. Once again an anthropomorphic example will be of some use. The sheet of paper on which I write is just that. Potentially it is a paper airplane, a libelous letter that could land me in jail, a shopping list, an opportunity for a sketch, and so on. It signifies; it is susceptible to, to use Whitehead's term, a "subjective aim." Because it is not disconnected from the actual world, it is a bundle of possible values (including negative ones). *Precisely because it is not a mere fact, it is potentially many values.* The same thing is true of the ingredient eternal object. In actuality it simply is, but taken independently of its actuality it has potential value. Its actual value will depend on what function it serves in the *new* actual occasion which utilizes it. "Mental experience is the organ of novelty," says Whitehead, "the urge beyond. It seeks to vivify the massive physical fact, which is repetitive, with the novelties which beckon" (*FR*, 26-27). It is, he says in the same work, "the experience of forms of definiteness [these are the "eternal objects" of the technical works] in respect to their disconnection from any particular physical experience, but with abstract evaluation of what they *can* contribute to such experience" (*FR*, 26).

The Function of Reason, from which these passages are taken, was published in the same year as *Process and Reality.* As lectures, these materials include popularizations of restricted themes from *Process and Reality.* The passages show two things: (1) Whitehead meant his basic principles to apply to the gross features of experience from which they draw their vocabulary, as well as to the microunits of reality, actual occasions; thus our "anthropomorphic" examples are not only analogies but examples. (2) The notions of evaluation, possibility, and mentality are intimately intertwined. We recall Whitehead's remark in *Science and the Modern World* that value is the name used for the "intrinsic" reality of an event. We turn then to the metaphysical roots of evaluation.

III   *The Category of Conceptual Valuation*

"Conceptual Valuation" is Whitehead's name for the fourth "Category of Obligation." First a word about the nine "obligations" generally. The word "obligation" is to be understood in its etymological sense. The nine categories of obligation are the ways in which the elements of the world are *bound together, lig*atured. The three previous categories refer to: (1) the essential unity and internal consistency of the prehensions which are bound together in one actual occasion ("Subjective Unity"), (2) the nonduplication of any element in the way it functions for some particular actual entity ("Objective Identity"), and (3) the converse relation, the nonidentity of any two elements, regardless of how similar their relation to the actual entity is ("Objective Diversity"). This fourth category is nothing but the rule that each physical feeling is accompanied by a conceptual feeling of the eternal object *qua object,* which is the basic mode—this conceptual feeling—of evaluation. "The subjective form of a conceptual feeling," says Whitehead, "has the character of a 'valuation' " (*PR,* 367). He goes on to explain that a conceptual feeling "arises in some incomplete phase of its subject and passes into a supervening phase in which it has found integration with other feelings."

There is nothing to prevent the actual occasion from using the eternal object exactly as it was antecedently used, that is, with minimum exploitation of novelty, sheer mimicry. But there is nothing in the previously objectified and completed actual occasion—nor in the eternal object itself, which as such is a sheer possible—to confine the reiteration of the eternal object to the same mode. The actual occasion makes itself, under the limitations of the available materials, and in the company of other processes like its own. Nor is it to be deplored that such repetition occurs. The stability of the world process lies in just this reliability of the largely physical order. Just as Whitehead says that "life is a bid for freedom," so he insists that mentality is the appearance of possible anarchy (see *FR,* 27; cf. *PR,* 163). All endurance, including mental endurance, is only some case or kind of the survival and transmission of dominantly repetitious pattern. Endurance is the limiting case of memory.

Whitehead means here to give credence to the medieval doctrine (itself resting on Aristotle's *De Anima*), that there is nothing in the intellect which was not first in the senses. But also, he means to give generalization and subtlety. For the doctrine now becomes, "There is nothing in concept that did not at first enter by way of a physical percept." The iron demand of actuality, that it be recognized for what it is, should not be used in the service of a determinism of either action or concept, however. For an actual occasion, by reason of its "subjective form," may see the eternal object in a quite different light from the way in which it was presented, while still acknowledging the "is-ness" of the presentation. Subjective form determines, not the eternal object, but its use.[1] And the use of the eternal object in turn demands its disengagement from the particular actual occasion in which it is ingredient. The result may be a "reversion."

IV   *The Category of Conceptual Reversion*

Once again, literal etymology for Whitehead's terms helps us through what might otherwise be a troublesome unfamiliarity. A reversion is nothing but a re-version, a new edition of our turning toward something. It is perilously close to a revision, and had that word not the sense of alteration, as "reviewing" has the sense of sheer restatement, it—or "reviewing"—might have been employed. Reversion is what happens when the unchanging eternal object is seen in another light, from another angle. So also traditional folk songs and tales are immortally part of our pasts. New versions arise, however. It is the newness Whitehead wants us to focus on. He says of reversion, "It is the category by which novelty enters the world" (*PR,* 381).

This passage is worth slow reading. Whitehead does not say that this category is the author or the wellspring of novelty. We must look to the creativity for that. He does not say that it is what elicits or draws out novelty. We shall later find that God is the attractive (not the coercive) agent (*PR,*   522-23).   But   it   is   the   *category*   by   which novelty enters the world. Novelty is a multileveled, many-faceted phenomenon. But when novelty becomes a clear-cut feature of the world process, it enters by this category. In Conceptual Reversion there is first a phase of conceptual reproduction. Then there arises the second phase in which "the proximate novelties" are those aspects of the eternal object which refer to its relations to other eternal objects, and therefore to possible actualizations with other eternal objects—but always under the restraints imposed by "physical incompatibles." This latter warning reminds us that our introductory theme of "hybrid prehensions" has not been dropped but only diversified. Hybrid prehensions, we recall, have conceptual feelings for their objects, and these conceptual feelings have, in turn, eternal objects as their objects. Thus, in the nature of the case, there must be a conceptual linkage between at least two actual occasions, one prior to the other in time. A "hybrid prehension" is the "transmission of mental feeling." From this actual transmission there arises the possibility of transmutation. "Thus pure, and hybrid, physical feelings, issuing into a single conceptual feeling, constitute the preliminary phase of this transmutation in the prehending subject. . . . Transmutation is the way in which the actual world is felt as a community, and is so felt in virtue of its prevalent order" (*PR*, 383). Reversion is the threshold over which novelty appears in the context of order. Transmutation—which is an extension of this novelty—creates community, which is to say that it introduces functions to be found only in relatively high-grade organisms. It soon becomes apparent that by "community" Whitehead is indicating interlocked actual occasions in enduring objects characterized by stable, transmitted patterns.

V *The Category of Transmutation (Categoreal Obligation VI)*

In some respects, this is the heart of Whitehead's theory of human perception; nonetheless the category is designed to include more than human perception. It is a mine of central Whiteheadian concepts, although relatives of the notion are to be found, in less speculative (I use the term approbatively) form in the earlier works of Bertrand Russell and C. D. Broad. It leads us to a discussion of simple location, misplaced concreteness, presentational immediacy, and causal efficacy, terms that span three of Whitehead's books (*Science and the Modern World, Symbolism,* and *Process and Reality*) and embrace the main features of his systematic philosophy. The theory is couched in an unfamiliar vocabulary, challenging even to professional philosophers. The short summary that follows risks losing the subtlety and scope of that vocabulary in the interests of clarifying it. We must first investigate transmutation in some detail.

Transmutation occurs when a conceptual feeling which is the same for a set of physical feelings referring to a group of actual occasions is integrated with those feelings to produce a single complex physical feeling. This single complex physical feeling is rightly regarded as objective and may apply to the nexus of similarly felt actual occasions treated in an integrated way. All the same, the transmutation is a phase in the integrating of the prehending actual occasion as it forms itself, and the subjective roots of this transmutative process must not be forgotten.

Stated more simply, an actual occasion may have a set of physical prehensions of other actual entities such that they collectively give rise to a common conceptual reproduction with the same eternal object for each of the various physical prehensions. "There will be only one direct conceptual feeling;" says Whitehead, "for the simple physical feelings (in the final subject) are analogous in the sense of exemplifying the same eternal object" (*PR,* 385). These transmuted physical feelings are "our usual way of consciously prehending the world" (*PR,* 387). He goes on to say that for human consciousness there is only one way of consciously prehending *single* actual entities, and that comes when we are consciously aware of other minds, "alien mentalities."

Human intelligence is most of the time engaged in a vast reductive simplification, dealing with masses of actual occasions. Only in the case of our elaborately mediated entry into another mind, in some single segment of its life, does our consciousness deal with a single actual occasion—and this itself a highly complex one. "The low-grade organism is merely the summation of the forms of energy which flow in upon it in all their multiplicity of detail. It receives, and it transmits; but it fails to simplify into intelligible system" (*PR,* 389).

Transmutation, says Whitehead, will thus generate a sensum which is "projected onto some external focal region defined by projectors" (*PR,* 493). In this passage Whitehead is dealing primarily with measurement and emphasizing the continuity and homogeneity of the continuum as the home of actual occasions and also as the theater in which our perception displays its data. He is, in other words, still following his task of undermining all attempts to divide nature perceived in ordinary experience from nature conceived in scientific discourse. Thus, the notion of sense data as "projected" receives no challenge, nor does it throughout the chapter dealing with the geometrical properties of space *(PR,* Pt. IV, Chapter 4). The reason is clear. If we isolate the geometrical properties of the continuum from the process that underlies them, any reference to nongeometrical properties in relation to this pure space and time presents these qualities as adventitiously laid on or into the continuum, as a painter impregnates a canvas.

But when Whitehead is dealing more concretely with process, prior to any isolation of its geometrical aspects, he protests the use of the idea of "projection" since it promotes a double illusion: that of an independent continuum and that of the exclusively subjective character of sense data. "In the usual language, the sensations are projected. This phraseology is unfortunate; for there never were sensations apart from these geometrical relations" *(PR,* p. 262). This is the more guarded statement and requires no qualification. The remark is made in the context of Whitehead's discussion of human perception. We are now in a position to discuss this complex type of prehension in its broad outlines.

VI   *The Problem of Human Perception*

The mind-body problem is most acute and familiar in respect of the problem of human perception. Let us try to review it briefly. Doing away with the notion of a world existing independently of human consciousness is rarely undertaken professionally, and never in popular philosophy. Certainly Whitehead did not undertake to do so. His respect for science included the conviction that it searches for order among things real. It is equally evident that the apprehension of this world by men is powerfully affected by their sensory, perceptual, and conceptual equipment. Variations in sensory mechanisms—color blindness, for example—or in perceptual habits—for example those suggested by the relatively late emergence of perspective in representational painting—warn us that there is a degree of variability in human perceptual sensation, over and above the variability of a surmised world.

Add to these human variables the conceptual ones, and our

awareness of reality seems to be so hopelessly coated over with adventitious data as to raise a question: in our apprehension of the world do we *ever* find *anything* given to us just as it is; don't we always tamper in the act of discovery? When we grasp the world, what do we find beyond the clutch-marks of our own hands? One of the greatest of philosophers, Kant, came to the conclusion that the thing-in-itself is inherently unknowable. The thrust of his conviction lies in a single premise: perceptual knowledge is a relation to its object, and we cannot know a thing both as it is related and as it is unrelated. What we know, then, are appearances, and all that is intelligible in appearance derives from the side of the knower. To be sure, I am aware of the independence of the world as it stands over against my will, my intent, and so on. But such practical awareness bears no marks of intelligibility and hence has no theoretical power, that is, power to permit me to form *theories* about the independent nature of the world. Whitehead condemns this view as holding that scientists are engaged either in constructing fairy tales or in peculiarly intricate autobiography.

Our common sense is strangely bankrupt in this matter. Is the green book still green in the lightless room? The usual answer is that it has a pigment that absorbs all but the green parts of daylight and related lights, reflecting the green only. The answer is useful, but vulnerable. This "transmission" theory of perception leaves me with a physical object over there which, under appropriate conditions, reflects light waves of a certain frequency. These are transmitted to my eye, the main target being the retina, a multireceptor organ equipped with ganglia which funnel the wave disturbance through the optic nerve and thence to my brain, in the optic lobes. Here some transmutation (I use Whitehead's word deliberately) occurs, which results in the appearance, not of the transmitting waves, but of an extended color patch; but the locus of this color patch is not given where it—according to the theory—occurs. The transmutation occurs in the brain, but the apparent location is in the unoffending book that bounced the filtered light back at me in the first place. The "real" "physical" object is over there, colorless, and my brain generated its own transmuted product, the green, back to the origin of the disturbance, neatly superimposing it.

But I cannot stop here. For the pages of the book follow the same course as the cover. By "page" I mean a piece of (generally) white paper. The pages are at the moment hidden. Surely the pages are not of no-color-at-all. Pages are of some color, but no color *occurs* without the sensing apparatus over here. So I am reduced to the so-called primary qualities of Locke: number, shape, size, and so on. Solidity? No, that goes too. Touch and sight agree the book is solid. But the X-ray does not confirm this. So the book is in one sense permeable and in another sense not. After all, says common sense, you cannot go through a fence, either. Yet the same fence does not stop an insect for long, if at all. Right, but that is not the question. I want to know if there is a *real* solidity out there or just a relative one (i.e., relative to me). If relative, then not independent, and the permeability to the X-ray is equally relative. So there is no solidity-in-itself.

This kind of analysis ultimately leaves us, in current scientific theory, with a reality "composed" of electromagnetic "fields" whose detection depends upon elaborately mediating technical equipment, and whose intelligibility rests upon measurement and an intricate body of theory built up with confirmational experiment.

The question arises: Can this "combination" (whatever that may mean) of these electromagnetic fields be called reality? Too much of what one ordinarily is justified in calling real has had to be relegated to secondary or tertiary status. Not only green and solidity, but joy, anger, love. From the purely "physical" point of view, color and emotion are at best derivative phenomena. But now I have talked my green book out of primary existence entirely, in spite of its evident status in my perception, in favor of merely reasoned entities, which I insist on calling "genuinely" real even though it is *they* who have been derived from the *perceptually given.* How can I justify this?

The problem could be continued further, for it has many aspects, but we stop here. For one thing, a complete analysis of the problem and Whitehead's method of dealing with it would occupy a separate book. Second, the present author's conviction is that such a final laying-to-rest of the problem was *not* accomplished by Whitehead. His approach is novel, exhibiting great consistency with the rest of his metaphysics. Moreover, it opens vistas of approach which may offer more opportunity for advance than familiar ones. If we can exhibit the general mode of answer and its basic assumptions, we will have covered enough.

The terms "transmutation" and "relative" have been deliberately employed, the former for obvious reasons. Let us turn to the notion of "relativity."

VII *Relativity and Presentational Immediacy*

Early in the rise of the scientific theory of relativity, Whitehead came to the conclusion that the principle of relativity extends far beyond the domain of a physical measurement.[2] This generalized theory of relativity can be stated quite simply: all existence is relative to other existence, as is all action, all becoming. Whitehead thus gets around the problem of the thing-in-itself by insisting not that we cannot *know* such things, but that they cannot *be.* This is his major move from epistemology to metaphysics.

On this view the electron, the green, and the emotion of aspiration have joint status in a common world of process. The problem is to elucidate the relations among these various types of entities, rather than undertaking to reduce them to one another—as for instance in the claim that anger is "nothing-but" a felt excess of adrenalin. It is the reductionism involved in the "nothing-but" approach that Whitehead wishes to avoid. Human perception is of course *relative* to human sense and human reason, but so is any physical action or state relative to antecedent states of the world. Both metaphysics and epistemology have been hampered by the conception of substance-quality as a primary mode of analysis. We begin by thinking of the basic units of the world process as *things* (independent substances), having characteristics (qualities), and undergoing adventures in a separate and distinct space and time. From this beginning we generate our problems. The green of the book is either a quality in the book or a quality in me. And if it is in the one place, how did it get there from where it was born? And is there even an "it" to get from one place to another: what is the "it" that is the same for a light wave of a certain frequency and a felt shade of green?

Whitehead's attack on the substance-quality conception of reality is an attack not on its veracity but on its concreteness. He is in no doubt about there being blue chairs, green books, and solid gray rocks. Nor is he in any doubt that it makes sense to deal with them as in some definite place or in some definite motion, and at or through some time.

His point is simple: judgments (asserted or not, it makes no difference here) of the world in terms of things that have certain characteristics and are merely related to space and time by being located somewhere are judgments that deal with *abstract entities.* No matter which way we go, into the precise inquiries of physical science or the direct deliveries of experience, we find not *things* (substances), but *events* as the primary ingredient. Under the strictures of scientific analysis the green book becomes a vast swarm of interconnected "fields." These fields are not static things but strings of occurrences. They are vibratory entities, activities. Even their boundaries are somewhat difficult to establish. Or if I go to perception, *at root* I find its primary ingredients are *also* events. The base fact in experience is my conscious-here-perceiving-those-characters-over-there-now. The hyphens symbolize the original togetherness of the mentality, the spatiality, the temporality, and the distinguishing characteristics. From this basic many-faceted experience, itself a complex event, certain abstractions can be made, for example: "the chair" (without reference to *me,* when, or where) or "the twenty feet of 'empty space' between the walls," and so on. The base-line fact is the experiential event related to other events. From this we extract objects and their qualities, spaces, times, relations, and so on.

In *Symbolism,* written after *Science and the Modern World* and before *Process and Reality* Whitehead explores this problem. Here he first develops his views on these points. Later, in *Process and Reality,* he changes the way in which he uses his vocabulary. For example, this statement could never have come from *Process and Reality:* "Personally I prefer to restrict mentality to those experiential activities which include concepts in addition to percepts" (*Sym,* 20). As we know, that preference was completely done away with, and the term "mental" was generalized to cover the minimum isolation of an eternal object by the nonphysical pole of any entity, however simple. But the major *themes* are the same. A sustained passage from the earlier book will serve as a good introduction to the complicated statement in *Process and Reality:*

...we do not perceive disembodied colour or disembodied extensiveness: we perceive *the wall's* colour and extensiveness. The experienced fact is "colour away on the wall for us." Thus the colour and the spatial perspective are abstract elements, characterizing the concrete way in which the wall enters into our experience.

Thus far, we notice the interlocking of qualitative, spatial, and conscious factors. Whitehead continues the passage, using the term "relational" where he other times speaks of relativity, and now introduces the temporal element:

They are therefore relational elements between the "percipient at that moment," and that other equally actual entity, or set of entities, which we call the "wall at that moment."

Here we see an early use of the idea of an actual entity. In *Process and Reality* the wall would unambiguously have to be a *set* of actual entities, whose multiple physical relations to the moment of consciousness fuse conceptually into a single conceptual feeling embodied in the grayness, say, of the wall. Its individual electromagnetic entities, in this moment of each of their lives, are not individually given for direct conceptual registry. And certainly no one of them is in itself gray. By the category of transmutation, collectively they conceptually register as gray; a single eternal object characterizes them all in their relation to the perceiving consciousness, itself related to the vast sensory apparatus in the organisms that support it. One kind of transmutation, then, is the massive reduction of awareness to a conceptually simple set of eternal objects. Whitehead now draws the distinction between "abstract" and "concrete," which not only continues the ideas developed in his analysis of "simple location" in *Science and the Modern World* (see chapter 6) but shapes so much of the thought of *Process and Reality*. The passage continues:

But the mere colour and the mere spatial perspective are very abstract entities, because they are only arrived at by discarding the concrete relationship between the wall-at-that-moment and the percipient-at-that-moment. This concrete relationship is a physical fact which may be very unessential to the wall and very essential to the percipient. The spatial relationship is equally essential both to wall and percipient: but the colour side of the relationship is at that moment indifferent to the wall, though it is part of the make-up of the percipient.

Quite clearly Whitehead here is having some trouble with what the term "wall" designates; he is making the proper concession to what must be called the "physical wall" as being something which may or may not be entering into a relational situation where a color-datum arises. The occurrence of that color-datum is a function of a multisided—a so-called polyadic—relation which has many terms in it, including the light conditions, the sensing apparatus of the perceiver, and so on. But this does not mean that the color experience is somehow less real than the abstractable objects to which it applies, and it does not mean that there is a later "projection" of the color data onto an uncolored wall. Whitehead has already said in a prior passage, "There are no bare sensations which are first experienced and then 'projected' into our feet as their feelings, or onto the opposite wall as its colour. The projection is an integral part of the situation, quite as original as the sense-data. . . . The use of the term 'wall' is equally misleading by its suggestion of information derived symbolically from another mode of perception" (*Sym.* 14). This other mode is called "causal efficacy." We shall examine it shortly, together with the other primary mode of perception, "presentational immediacy." Meanwhile, the passage we are examining concludes as follows:

In this sense, and subject to their spatial relationship, contemporary events happen independently. I call this type of experience "presentational immediacy." It expresses how contemporary events are relevant to each other, and yet preserve a mutual independence. . . . This presentational immediacy is only of importance in high-grade organisms, and is a physical fact which may, or may not, enter into consciousness. Such entry will depend on attention and on the activity of conceptual functioning, whereby physical experience and conceptual imagination are fused into knowledge. (*Sym,* 15-16)

This last section is easily swallowed whole without digestion. Let us chew it a bit. We notice that Whitehead says of "presentational immediacy" that it is a "physical fact." It is just as real, just as actual, as any of the events which contribute to it. It is no more temporary than they; *Process and Reality* presents actual occasions as both concrete and quite brief. Presentational immediacy is not illusory. The temptation is to say, "Yes, but it is largely subjective." This is clearly the kind of consideration that led Whitehead to ask himself in *Process and Reality* if he should not also regard the least units of existence as having a "subjective" aspect, and a "mental" pole, however simple. If homogeneity between the human and the nonhuman (which is presumed in the fact that persons have knowledge of things) is to be explained, on Whitehead's view, it will not be by trying to reduce mind to matter (materialism) or matter to mind (idealism), but by discerning the mental elements and the physical elements in all *basic* existence. In this way we not only have a suitable basis for the interrelation between the two but also a foundation for allowing the gradual evolutionary emergence of life from nonlife, and consciousness from nonconsciousness.

The other item to be underscored is the relatively simple way in which Whitehead has here, in this brief work, introduced what will later, in *Process and Reality,* be called transmutation. He speaks of "conceptual functioning, whereby physical experience and conceptual imagination are fused into knowledge."

To summarize the subject of relativity: Concrete existence is relational. Things exist by reason of their relations to other things. Moreover, concrete existence is time-structured; time is essential to it, not adventitious. Contemporaneity, for example, gives us relatively independent entities, but they tap back to common ancestors—the intricated events of the antecedent world. From contemporary events not immediately and wholly dependent upon one another, we can distill off abstract objects with their qualities, or conscious selves for that matter. And these two kinds of "substance," mental and physical, can then be discerned as having certain kinds of inherent quantities. This distillation ignores the experiential and eventlike character of the world, delivering somewhat static independent things, "substances," and ignores their joint emergence from the events of the past, upon whose existence they are directly dependent. These themes can be filled out if we pay attention to the other perceptual mode, "causal efficacy," and to a third mode of experience, the fusion product of causal efficacy and presentational immediacy, "symbolic reference." As an introduction to these three modes, we shall briefly consider "simple location" as discussed in *Science and the Modern World.*

CHAPTER 6

Body and Mind (B):
Causation and Perception

I   *Misplaced Concreteness and Mere Location*

The main difficulty with the substance-quality metaphysics is that the evidence for it is secondary. We start out with those simplified elements of our experience which are the first things that we are normally interested in—a world of things. But the beginning point of our perceptual interest is not necessarily the beginning point of our perceptual engagement with the world. It is natural for us to look at the world as populated by objects with locations and characteristics.

At the moment I am looking at a small copper teapot. It is shiny, copper colored, sitting on a shelf a few feet away. The mode of perception here is automatic, reinforced by thousands of years of usefulness, and unchallengeably practical. But there are risks in this way of perceiving. I am all too likely to extend the mode of thought to the analysis of human selves—which are not objects of immediate sensory perception—or of whatever current candidates there are for the status of "ultimate scientific objects," which are likewise not given to such perception. But there is a further difficulty. Speaking concretely, that is, leaving nothing out that is pertinent, the substance-quality mode of analysis will not even adequately account for the perceived world.

The teapot itself is abstract. If I go to my evidence for it, I inevitably come upon my percipient self as a highly germane factor. A shift of position produces a different color, or color blindness may deny me the common experience of that color. Illness, or a temporarily or

109

permanently distorted eyeball will give a different shape, and so on.
The root empirical fact is of a perceptual occasion, part of whose
controls seem to be "over here" and part "over there." The appearance
of the sense data radically depend on me over here, although they
inhabit the object over there. As we have seen before, if I do not
develop a theory of knowledge which takes into account this multiple
relationship, I wind up with an epistemology whose best strength lies in
its possibility of defeating other ones. The clue can be extracted from
the word "appearance" used above. The base fact of experience—if we
are to be consistent empiricists—is that the experience itself is a chain
of occurrences, including appearances. An "appearance" is an
occurrence, an event. Derivatively, we may speak of the appearance of
the pot—for example, "What is its general appearance?"—but this is a
summation of average reliable past-events with expectation of more
appearances to come. The repetition of patterns of appearance leads us
to leave their times, and our own roles in the appearances, out of the
statement and out of account. The result is an abstract substance,
merely existing. Such a substance has mere location. That is, sheer
location is an adequate spatiotemporal account of how substances exist.
But it is not an adequate account of the prehensive experience from
which they have been abstracted. The error, Whitehead says, is "an
example of what I will call the 'Fallacy of Misplaced Concreteness' "
(*SMW*, 74-75). In the point of fact, "The sense-object [for example, the
copper color of the illustration above] is present in A [the percipient
event] with the mode of location in B [the perceived event] " (*SMW*,
103). For a concrete actual occasion, mere location is but one property
in a complex relationship.[1] When a sense-object ingresses, it does so
over there as being known, and over here as constituting an element in
the actual occasion which is some segment of the life of an enduring
object, the perceiver. This theme is repeated and amplified in *Process
and Reality*. Whitehead says there that an eternal object functions "both"
"as a determinant of the datum and as a determinant of the subjective
form . . . In this sense the solidarity of the universe is based on the
relational functioning of eternal objects" (*PR*, 249). A cautionary note
should be added to this remark. Whitehead's language, by his own
standards, is a bit loose here. Primary agency is that which arises in the
self-causation of an actual occasion. Strictly, it is the actual occasion

which, acting under the category of transmutation, introduces the two-way functioning sense-object in its dual role. This fact warrants the guarded use of the idea of "projection," as we have already observed.

II *Presentational Immediacy and Causal Efficacy*

Briefly, then, we may say that the presentational immediacy, which we encountered in the previous chapter, simplifies what is illustrated in it (according to the category of transmutation) and focuses its attention on the world rendered vivid in perception. There should be no quarrel with this almost exclusively "automatic" procedure. But there is a warning that it is but one mode of perceptual experience, and being thus limited in its scope, it gives us no models for metaphysical generality. *Specula* built in such narrow valleys will reveal only a distorted and paradoxical landscape. One further remark needs to be appended here. Presentational immediacy cannot err. It makes no judgments. Properly employed, it merely immediately presents dream, delusion, or the actual; it makes no difference; presentational immediacy is their common domain; it makes no mistakes, because it makes no claims. It merely serves up data. We must look elsewhere if we seek for the origins of error.

Presentational immediacy is but one mode of perception, however. The other is the "vague, but insistent" *causal efficacy.*

Hume had searched in vain for the warrant for our feelings of certainty about the causal relationship. There is a logical necessity in the terms "cause" and "effect"—namely, that each carries implicative meaning for the other. But this does not help us in our effort to use the terms properly. If we go to our experience, he says, we find no warrant either. We do find sequences of paired events such that when A happens, then B follows, but how, says Hume, do we jump to the conclusion that whenever A, then necessarily B? It is quite thinkable without logical offense that a rock should disappear on contact or be replaced by three elves in shirt sleeves. Fairy stories abound with princes who emerge from kissed frogs. What is offended is not logic but our habits of experience. Yet experience is never done, is full of surprises, and is our only primary source of knowledge. Finally, we look in vain for some ingredient that passes from the thrown rock to the broken glass, from the light switch or the wire to the glowing lamp. Power? Force? Energy? This is circular: the evidence for them lies in the chains of events which validate their alleged presence. If they are supported by these sequences of events, their names are useless for supporting the idea of cause in the events. They do not name occult properties; we have only our repeated associations of past experience to warrant even our practical employment of these terms.

And that is as far as we can go with causality, according to Hume. We should be idle indeed to doubt the *practical* usefulness of the concept of causality, he says. But practical usefulness is a far cry from theoretical reasoning, with its pretense of invulnerability. From the standpoint of theory, our only account of causality must be that its alleged necessity is quite subjective. What we really have is a custom, a habit, of linking together events which have been associated in the past, and from this we fall into regarding them as necessarily so linked. But the history of ordinary knowledge and scientific understanding is littered with discarded "necessities" of this sort. Experience outruns theory, and even where it doesn't, we cannot say it won't.

The shrewd criticism of the causal relationship did much to clear out complacent dead thoughts in philosophy. Kant says Hume woke him "from his dogmatic slumber." But, according to Whitehead, Hume's weakness lies largely in his dwelling on presentational immediacy alone. If we search through the contents of what we perceive, Hume's argument seems invulnerable.[2] And this searching through the *contents* of perception is what passed for empiricism from the time of Hume to that of James. With William James comes the analysis of experience with as little presupposition as possible, so that empiricism now means, not just the analysis of *what* is experienced but of the experiencing *process* itself. This "radical empiricism," as James called it, found an advocate and metaphysical promoter in Whitehead, whose originality is confluent with James's here.

No recherché data are needed. What is needed is that we leave off looking in the same place to which Hume confined himself. Even Hume is led to analyze the process of experience, and then a quite different tale unfolds, a more complex one which at least partially reinstalls causality as a fundamental relationship rather than as a construct supported only by its practical usefulness. Hume tells us that "sensations arise in the soul from unknown causes." This is Hume's "make-believe," says Whitehead (*PR,* 259), where Hume is maintaining his skeptical posture. (Whitehead spares us the obvious comment that even this is too much, since it asserts causes). But when Hume gets down to actual analysis, he drops his ignorance. He says, "If it be perceived by the eyes, it must be a color; if by the ears, a sound; if by the palate, a taste; and so of the other senses" (*PR,* 181; cited from *Treatise of Human Nature,* Pt. I, Sect. VI). Here the necessary organs as causative controls are wisely admitted. Consciousness, sensory organs, enduring objects "out there": this is the minimum triad of the perceptual relationship, at least for human beings.

It is fruitless to deny the necessity of cause when you find causal factors assumed in order to explain the perception which never has causes in its contents. If we dwell on what is vividly present in presentational immediacy, Hume's claim looks good, but if we investigate how presentational immediacy comes about, we soon find ourselves giving a causal analysis. The dogma "that all percepts are in the mode of presentational immediacy" is simply not true, Whitehead says (*PR,* 266). All perception has in it the sense of the " 'withness' of the body" (*PR,* 125). There are ignored and suppressed, "vague but insistent" data that *are* percepts although they are not given in presentational immediacy. The sense of eyestrain in seeing is not itself seen but felt in the *effort* to see. The camera analogy for the eye will not do. Eyes, ears, tactic organs work. They do something. But even in relative passivity their third-term role is evident. A man who has been made to blink by a flash is not likely to accept the Humean account of causality. That account of this "making" would be that first there was the perception of the flash, then the perception of the blink. Enough repetitions of this sequence then persuade us that there is a necessary cause operating. But the Humean explanation is artificial and implausible here for a simple reason. The man himself has been party to the transaction. He does not need to judge reflectively; he has *felt directly* the flash as a cause. (*PR,* 365-66).

One more feature of Whitehead's multifaceted attack on Hume's theory of cause:[3] it is not so much an argument as it is a bid for consistency in how we view the world. It concerns evolution, whose main features Whitehead never doubted. As we go down the scale of complexity of living forms, we soon find a sharp diminution in the "variety of sense-presentation, and then vivid distinctness of presentational immediacy," but the awareness of causal relationships seems to persist in the behavior of these less complex living things. Even a "jellyfish advances and withdraws, and in so doing exhibits some perception of causal relationship with the world beyond itself" (*PR*, 268). Whitehead does not say it here, but the implication is clear. Even when we get to the simplest unitary elements, the least actual occasions, the rule is still present: causal *constitution* of one entity because of the antecedent presence of others. In high-grade organisms the mode of presentational immediacy becomes dominant, pressing the inarticulate sense of causal efficacy toward the margins of consciousness (*PR*, 261-64 passim). "It must be remembered that clearness in consciousness is no evidence for primitiveness in the genetic process: the opposite doctrine is more nearly true" (*PR*, 263-64). Thus it is that symbolic reference, which represents the "intersection" of the two modes of perception (*Sym*, 49), often seems to deal with the data of presentational immediacy. For example, "Language almost exclusively refers to presentational immediacy as interpreted by symbolic reference" (*PR*, 263).

III   *Symbolic Reference*

For there to be an intersection between the two modes requires that they share some aspects of perception. There are two such aspects: (1) sense data and (2) locality (*Sym*, 49).

First, we must keep in mind that Whitehead is insisting that the perceived world is as much a part of the real world as is the reasoned world. For one thing, it is through the data of perception that we gain the materials for reasoning. If we reason to what "underlies" these data, we can hardly come up with answers which deny the reality of our original means of entry to the unperceived. Nevertheless, the data of perception are in some sense adventitious to the organisms on which they are "projected." The sense data arise completely and causally, by reason of the antecedent state of that which appears as colored, for instance, but also by reason of the antecedent state of the perceiving (human) body. "The sense-data, required for immediate sense-perception, enter into experience in virtue of the efficacy of the environment.

This environment includes the bodily organs" (*Sym,* 52). And where the sense data are felt to be, they are, because presentational immediacy merely presents. But where they are means—location. Sight is comparatively precise—sound and smell less so, but they include directional cues, at least enough to distinguish them from the localizations of touch and taste; yet even these have, of course, localization. The sweet taste, though *of* the sugar, is *in* my mouth. The pain or pressure is *in* my knee. The sound comes from (vaguely mayhap) "over there." The red book is four and a half feet away, in that direction. No doubt the acute localization given by sight adds force to skepticism about causes. In sight we have the acutest cases of apparent-separation-from-perceiver and spatial discreteness. Sense data and space both seem here remarkably detached from us. But as we turn to the other sense, the "withness" of the body gains in prominence. We say, only rarely, "Is that redness in my eyes or in the house?" But we often say, "Is that ringing in my ears or in the radiator?" Sometimes we say, "I have a ringing in my ears." The situation has already been localized and prejudged. Smell seems no less external in its origin but less so as to location. Taste, though it "objectifies" (to use Whitehead's word) the sugar as surely as the red does the rose, is much more intimate. And in the various modes of touch, localization of data, locale, and subject are quite proximate. Finally, with physical pain and pleasure the interiority and hence "subjectivity" of the data and the locale are at their most acute.

In Whitehead's behalf, and on a point where he is both somewhat vulnerable (at least in the way he makes his point) and somewhat misunderstood, I have ranged sensory data from the most external to the most internal. I have suggested that this external-internal scale is rather close to the objective-subjective scale, insofar as we confine ourselves to the *sensorily given.* In every case, we have a sensory datum given with a location. These two links bind together presentational immediacy and causal efficacy. What has it to offer that presentational immediacy does not? The vividness and spatial definiteness of presentational immediacy lures us into thinking of it as the only source of "perception." The answer is *temporality.* Presentational immediacy gives us vivid glimpses of a constantly lapsing reality. But our sense of our own existence and of the world outruns this lapsing.

Whitehead's remarks on this point in *Symbolism* are largely confined to comments on time:

Time is known to us as the succession of our acts of experience, and thence derivatively as the succession of events objectively perceived in those acts. But this succession is not pure succession: it is the derivation of state from state, with the later state exhibiting conformity to the antecedent. Time in the concrete is the conformation of state to state, the later to the earlier; and the pure succession [of Hume, for example] is an abstraction from the irreversible relationship of settled past to derivative present. (*Sym,* 35)

Shortly he continues by saying that we "never doubt" this conformation, in practice, and that it "belongs to the ultimate texture of experience" just as clearly as does presentational immediacy.   (*Sym,* 46).

In *Process and Reality* the fuller doctrine emerges, the appeal is not merely to time and conformation but to the inescapable sense of existence, with the clearest example being self-existence. Here Whitehead emphasizes not only the sheer conformation to and derivation from the past, but the elements of emotion and the future, thus directing our attention even more acutely to personal existence. Causal efficacy, he says,

produces the sense of derivation from an immediate past, and of passage to an immediate future; a sense of emotional feeling, belonging to oneself in the past, passing into oneself in the present, and passing from oneself in the present towards oneself in the future; a sense of influx of influence from other vaguer presences in the past, localized and yet evading local definition, such influence modifying, enhancing, inhibiting, diverting, the stream of feeling which we are receiving, unifying, enjoying, and transmitting. This is our *general sense of existence,* as one *item* among others, in an efficacious actual world.

By diversion of attention we can inhibit its entry into consciousness; but, whether mentally analyzed or no, it remains the given uncontrolled basis upon which our character weaves itself. Our bodies are largely contrivances whereby some central actual occasion may inherit these basic experiences of its antecedent parts. (*PR,* 271; italics mine)

The greatest strength of Whitehead's view here is in his appeal to the immediate sense of personal continuity, personal endurance, which is not and could not be adequately satisfied or accounted for by sheer presentational immediacy. This is a form of Whitehead's insistence that endurance is the minimal case of causation. The endurance of any present state is the outcome of its quite close-grained repetition of past patterns. Where the skeptic may wish to argue is in the transfer of this sense of conformation to nonpersonal states. But this would be to put a wall of doubt between one's own existence and that of the perceived world. Such a skepticism is precisely what George Santayana attacks in *Scepticism and Animal Faith*.[4] Santayana's own skepticism then turns to skepticism itself, insofar as that skepticism tends toward solipsism, toward allowing as real and reliable only one's own existence. Santayana points out that willingness to accept one's own existence as the only certain existence, with the rest of the world given only as a kind of three-dimensional cinema, is incomplete. For such existence makes assumptions about one's personal past as real though not present, and these are just as dubitable as the assumptions about the external world. Santayana's point is that the skepticism which doubts existence other than itself cannot stop there. Why should one's past not also be an object of doubt—why have faith in one's prior existence and not a present independent world? The doubt, in short, about externality extends to temporal externality. One is then reduced to what Santayana calls the Selipsism of the Present Moment. Then, how small is the moment? Whitehead evidently takes this argument as definitive (it is difficult not to) and repeatedly refers his readers to it (*PR*, 240; *Sym*, 28-29). Whitehead's constructive alternative to this skepticism is not "animal faith," however, but the analysis we have been following, for which he says drily he "cannot claim Santayana's authority" (*Sym*, 29).

It should be noticed in passing that Whitehead is virtually alone among modern philosophers, independent of the current fusion of existentialism and phenomenology, in emphasizing the "withness of the body," which is a *perceptum*, lacking the vividness of perception as ordinarily understood, but discernible as present through all perception. Sartre and Merleau-Ponty, to mention only two of the most widely known examples, both have sustained treatments of the body and its role in existence.[5] Like these philosophers, Whitehead argues, in *Process and Reality*, from the causal factor in one's own sense of existence—he dresses this sense in the vocabulary of "inheritance"—to the existence, with its causal factors, of the contemporary world. In brief, one cannot imagine (or, I think Whitehead would say, even discuss) a world in community with a self, in which the causal factor in endurance stops with one's own self-existence and is replaced by mere sequence in the case of the presented world. For one thing, where is the boundary between self and world?

We have come full circle to the subject of relativity, in its generalized sense. Scientific relativity is concerned with problems of measurement in inertial systems in motion relative to one another. It focuses on the quantitative features of observational experience, the qualitative being only vehicles for them. Whitehead's generalized treatment refuses to brush aside these qualitative features as mere vehicles. His target is more than the relativity of measurable inertial systems. "Ultimately all observation, scientific or popular, consists in the determination of the spatial relation of the bodily organs of the observer to the location of 'projected' sense-data" (*Sym,* 56). The formal statement of the principle of relativity is given in *Process and Reality* in a formal way. It is Category iv of the "Categories of Explanation":

> That the potentiality for being an element in a real concrescence of many entities into one actuality, is the *one general metaphysical character* attaching to all entities, actual and non-actual; and that every item in the universe is involved in each concrescence. In other words, it belongs to the nature of a "being" that it is a potential for every "becoming." This is the "principle of relativity." (*PR,* 33; italics mine)

I have italicized the central term in the above phrase to call attention to it. Another way of looking at this notion is to say "irrelevance" between any two entities is a sign that those entities have been (perhaps for very good reasons) abstractly regarded.

Symbolic reference thus, by being the "intersection" of our two modes of perception, exposes us to interconnections between ourselves and the world, which presentational immediacy obscures. Our difficulty arises from a mistake that is all too easy to make. We follow Hume's explicit doctrine (rather than his implicit assumptions) in looking for one kind of perception in the domain of another. We search, that is, for causes and effects in sheer immediacy. But our most insistent awareness of causality, and therefore our best evidence, is in the primary and felt continuities of our existence. Whitehead calls this "inheritance," basic causal transmission. It is the business of presentational immediacy to illuminate some complex, contemporary features of this process of inheritance, *not* to exhibit this inheritance as the outcome of customarily associated acts.

The subject of symbolic reference opens up the analysis of consciousness and hence what Whitehead calls the "Higher Phases of Experience."

CHAPTER 7

Consciousness

Since Whitehead believes in the gradual emergence of consciousness, founded upon perception, it is somewhat arbitrary as to where to start. Already the subject has appeared repeatedly—as it should—in the analysis of perception. But if we distinguish between perceptive consciousness and reflective consciousness, and for the moment reserve "consciousness" for the latter phenomenon, we come abruptly to "propositions."

Whitehead's innovations in the theory of propositions, in *Process and Reality,* are perhaps not so far-reaching as some of his less flagrantly stated doctrines. But they are easily the most startling. The master of formal logic, who, with his former student Bertrand Russell, initiated the English-speaking world into formal logic, giving that world its most comprehensive treatise (in three large volumes) on the subject, has something entirely new, in his cosmology, to say about propositions. To begin with, he assigns them locations. This officially exiled him from the camp of his logician followers but aroused the interests of philosophers of broader interest. "Propositions" in *Process and Reality,* constitute a special category of existence, the sixth. They are said to be "Matters of Fact in Potential Determination, *or* Impure Potentials for the Specific Determination of Matters of Fact, *or* Theories" (*PR,* 32-33).

From this wordy label let us abstract "Impure." Had the term "hybrid" not been given a technical meaning—as an important kind of prehension—we might call propositions "hybrids." They are not only hybrids in the sense that they are crosses between actual events (occasions or nexūs) and eternal objects, but also in the sense that they lie "between the beginning" of the synthesis of physical and conceptual

120

feelings and "the end of the integration into consciousness." Propositions are a good introduction to Whitehead's theory of consciousness because, although a propositional feeling does not of itself involve consciousness, still "Consciousness belongs to the subjective forms of such feelings" (*PR*, 391).

I *The Ontology of Propositions*

Whitehead limits himself to the logic of subject-predicate propositions. Two ends are thus served: (1) It is relatively simple and can serve as a good working model. The only signs we have of a relational logic are in the *Method of Extensive Connection,* Whitehead's account of the derivation of geometrical entities from the experienced world. This subject can not be profitably entered into here. (2) Moreover, our normal human judgments, with their deep-seated tendency toward reification, are commonly founded on the simplification which a subject-predicate logic introduces. The sense-datum, red, as we have seen, is itself a datum, arising through a transmuted feeling. "There are," says Whitehead, "limits to this handiness of the sense-data: but they are emphatically the manageable elements in our perceptions of the world" (*Sym,* 56).

But there is a third good reason for the consideration of a subject-predicate logic. If a proposition be treated as having a locus, if it be tied to some "Matter-of-fact," if it—in short—have a location, then insofar it is *already* abstract. We recall that to be "merely located" is a property of material things in the traditional sense—that is, discernible objects residing in space and time with more or less distinctive characteristics. Presentational immediacy vivifies, segments, "object"-ifies the world, passing over the deeper-lying continuities to which our experience of causal efficacy gives only mute and vague acknowledgment. Indeed, conscious judgment issuing in sentences that embody propositions goes even further in analytic clarity. Perception may yield the presence of a round, green pot over there. Two propositions—"The pot is round" and "The pot is green"—are available. They have a common locus, and independent predicates. For example, the truth or falsity of one proposition does not involve that of the other. The subject of the proposition always designates an actuality, for example, the vase characterized by tangible qualities. The predicate designates an alleged characteristic as being actualized in the actuality designated by the subject. Thus, "every proposition must be somewhere. The 'locus' of a proposition consists of those actual occasions whose actual worlds include the logical subjects of the proposition" (*PR*, 283).

Let us stop here and assess, briefly. Bertrand Russell spent a lot of time worrying about propositions concerning the "Present King of France." For example, the falsity of the proposition "The present king of France is bald" would seem to require logically that "The present king of France is not bald" be true, which in turn seems to acknowledge the existence of a present king of France. He induced others to worry about this problem also, mainly logicians. The so-called theory of descriptions was developed to evade the difficulties of having true (or false) propositions about intelligible but nonexistent entities. Whitehead takes a direct and simpler route. The stipulation is clear: "Don't call it a proposition unless it deals with an actuality." Within the logical framework alone it was convenient for Russell and others to extend the term "proposition" to assertions including terms where there is no guarantee of the existence of designata for the terms. But the troublesome problem of *existential* truth, as opposed to logical truth, arises. Whitehead builds the existential requirement into a *narrowed* definition of propositions, rather than inventing a solution to the paradoxes that arise from the broader usage. After that he followed the implications of his procedure with ruthless consistency. The result is that a proposition—since it *must* have an existing subject-referent— has a *necessarily* ontological status associated with what it designates. Yet if we are to preserve the conventional notion of truth and falsity as applying to propositions, the whole of a proposition can hardly apply to actuality. A proposition would then always be true, and the subject of truth and falsity would have to move to some other terrain. Propositions would then be at best the invariable valid foundation of verbal photographs of reality.

In point of fact, in spite of Whitehead's unusual treatment of propositions, his position is reached by means quite in agreement with common sense. For example, if I say, "the coelocanths off Madagascar are all lighter than the water in which they live," the truth or falsity of this claim is not thought to rest upon whether or not there are coelocanths. No matter that someone may not know that they have indeed been found there. There is nothing logically untoward in someone's saying, in this situation, "I didn't know coelocanths still existed." And indeed, if the rejoinder came, "I didn't say there were any," it is unlikely that anyone would suppose that a serious point—or any point—in the domain of logic had been made. Verification of the proposition would rest in getting as many coelocanths as possible and seeing.

Now, if we mean business about this customary mode of claim and verification, then there are implied directives in the subject of the proposition. The subject of the proposition is no more arbitrary than the entity it designates. And indeed, we must now let go of ordinary usage and eliminate the word "designates." Strictly, the subject of the proposition *is* an actual entity, or more commonly a nexus of actual entities. "These actual entities are the logical subjects of the proposition" (*PR*, 393). Propositions themselves "are the tales that perhaps might be told about particular activities" (*PR*, 392). In greater detail, "a proposition, while preserving the indeterminateness of an eternal object, makes an incomplete abstraction from determinate actual entities (*PR*, 392-93). "But the proposition, in itself, apart from recourse to these reasons [see following paragraph], tells no tale about itself; and in this respect it is indeterminate like the eternal objects" (*PR*, 393). When a sentence frames or represents a proposition, then, it is the proposition which is to be tested, and what is tested is whether or not the eternal object—a sheer possibility—is actually an ingredient in an actual occasion or a nexus of occasions. The latter are determinate.

Whitehead himself—and this is a warning of the universal and unelaborated treatment of propositions—uses the language of reference as well, in speaking of propositions:

A proposition shares with an eternal object the character of indeterminateness, in that both are definite potentialities *for* actuality with undetermined realization *in* actuality. But they differ in that an eternal object refers to actuality with absolute generality, whereas a proposition refers to indicated logical subjects. Truth and falsehood always require some element of sheer givenness. Eternal objects cannot demonstrate what they are except in some given fact. The logical subjects of a proposition supply the element of givenness requisite for truth and falsehood. (*PR*, 395)

The reasons mentioned above must be *ontological* reasons, not just logical, semantic, or syntactic reasons. As Whitehead says, "according to the ontological principle (the seventeenth 'category of explanation') a reason is always a reference to determinate actual entities" *(PR,* 392). We notice here again the language of "reference," shortly followed by a summary statement: "The proposition is the possibility of *that* predicate applying in that assigned way to *those* logical subjects" *(PR,* 394).

One of the by-products, but an essential one, of Whitehead's procedure is to minimize somewhat the issue of truth and falsity of propositions. Whitehead says, "in the real world it is more important that a proposition be interesting than that it be true. The importance of truth is, that it adds to interest" *(PR,* 395-96; cf. 281). He might well have added the same thing of a falsity. This would constitute, then, a special application of his remark that "The triumph of consciousness comes with the negative intuitive judgment" *(PR,* 417). Elsewhere Whitehead points out that consciousness is more than the mere entertaining of theory; it is awareness of theory as theory (we recall that one name for a proposition is "theory") and of fact as fact, and the contrast between them, "whether or no the theory be correct" *(PR,* 286). We see (1) why the proposition must have a locus, namely, otherwise, its factual credibility is in question, and (2) why the hybrid prehensions from which consciousness rises must have both physical and conceptual elements in them.

II *Propositions and Judgments*

We have been examining the ontological status of propositions— peculiar entities indeed. They have a locus; the locus, however, does not hold all that they are. They are theories. Their truth or falsity rests on whether the eternal objects specified in their predicates are present in actuality. But more important than their truth or falsity is whether or not they are interesting. Why this? Roughly, the answer is that "The proposition is an element in the lure for feeling of an actual entity" *(PR,* 283). Propositions "are not primarily for belief, but for feeling at the physical level of unconsciousness" *(PR,* 283-84).

1. *Propositions as lures.* It is actual entities that entertain

propositions. They may do so conformally, that is, in such a way that the feeling of the new entity-in-process conforms to the available fact. Total conformity is unknown, says Whitehead. But in sheer physical endurance the uniform repetition of vibration in simple physical particles is close to total conformity. Or they may do so, nonconformally, realizing some novelty inherent in what the proposition reveals by way of its reference to eternal objects. Nonconformity introduces the possibility of error, disorder, and so on, but it is the precondition of growth, which brings novelty into the prevailing order without serious disruption. Decay, as well as growth, may represent such nonconformity, where there is an "elimination of all dominant elements of feeling . . . [and] the route [the actual occasions constituting the life of an organism collectively] soon loses its historic individuality" (*PR*, 286).

2. *Propositions as founded on judgment.* Propositions constitute one of the eight major categories of existence. We are tempted therefore to think of them as having to be simply accepted for what they are. Whitehead, however, treats them as resting upon activities in the internal process of an actual entity which are "prior" to their appearance. These activities are those of judgment. A full-scale plunge into "judgments" would not result in abbreviating and simplifying *Process and Reality,* however. It would mean expanding. We must deal with a simple example: "A conscious perception is a very simplified type of affirmative intuitive judgment" (*PR,* 417).

The main distinction between a judgment and the proposition that is founded on it is that a judgment is a feeling, a synthetic feeling, and is therefore particular to some actual occasion; a proposition, however, can be the content for quite diverse judging subjects (*PR,* 293). Thus while a proposition is independent in the sense that it exists whether or not there are propositional feelings directed toward it, it is quite inoperative unless there be some judgment which seizes upon it. The judgment "is a decision of feeling, the proposition is what is felt . . ." *(ibid.).*

In speaking of "intuitive judgments" Whitehead is harking back to a philosophy which he is clearly reacting against: that of Immanual Kant. Kant too held that judgments are the synthetic elements which weave our sensory data into intelligible objects, the whole process under a strict regimen of twelve categories. Judgment is, then, the direct contact between self and appearance. The same conviction holds for Whitehead. Our intuitive judgments are judgments built into our intuition—where the term "intuition" means, as it does in Kant, the means through which sense operates. Such synthesis presides over any deliberate propositional formulation and indeed, for both men, provides the groundwork for it. But there is a double-barreled difference. In Kant judgment is a generic term, wherever we find a priori synthetic judgments, at least. These judgments are the same for all rational beings and not the private content of some particular perception or percipient. Indeed, for Kant, it is through such invariant forms of judgment that science is possible. Moreover, for Kant the thing-in-itself is unknowable, ultimately remote, and by definition inaccessible. For Whitehead, on the other hand, the independent physical world is knowable directly by symbolic reference. In symbolic reference there is a double reference, in causal efficacy and presentational immediacy, which provides a bridge between the simplified and vivid realm of appearance and the basic continuity, causally felt, between man and nature.

If we are to give examples of intuitive judgments, we must discuss cases which either are not propositionally formulated or require no such formulation (even if such there be). A man who reaches for a doorknob does so by reason of convictions derived from previous actual occasions. These provide data for the present—open—actual occasion, the judgment that the doorknob is actual, in working order, and so on. Any one of these judgments may be wrong, of course. The possibility of error extends into the sheer givenness of presentational immediacy (*PR,* 390). But what concerns us here is the quality of the judgment. It is of the yes-form. There are, secondly, judgments of the no-form. I do not go to the refrigerator for a bottle of beer. I "know" the refrigerator has none. Here too I could be wrong. Finally, there is the suspense-form (*PR,* 412-13), which intuitively presents the "yes" and "no" as not given. There is a wide range of such judgments. Basically, they rest on the idea of compatibility. Nothing in our experience blocks us from entertaining them, yet nothing conclusively verifies them either. If, for example, past experience suddenly urges on me the frequent providence of a thoughtful wife, the "beer in the refrigerator" judgment will come through labeled "maybe, maybe not." Then my *action* is different from the no-form, much more similar to what would have followed from the yes-form. But with this difference: emotions of rage, disappointment, and frustration will not attend a negative validation. "Our whole progress," says Whitehead, "in scientific theory, and even in subtility of direct observation, depends on the use of suspended judgments" (*PR,* 419). Zoologists for years regarded barnacles as mollusks. They based their conviction on the status of morphological analysis. A switch to the dynamics of embryological and genetic analysis showed the free-swimming larvae to be those of arthropods. The case is a classic of re-examination of the familiar, with increased "subtlety of direct observation."

But suspended judgment does not necessarily lead to investigative or re-investigative action. There may be great indifference, as well as indecision, on the yes-no problem. We then have "conscious imagination," and there stretch before us all those realms of truth, which Whitehead obviously does not investigate here, and which are not subject to literal verification or falsification, yet can be said to be veridical in their presentation. As an example, consider epic literature. Some of Homer seems to be quite literally true. "Yes" judgments about the *Iliad* spurred the dream and successfully focused the life of Heinrich Schliemann, but the *Iliad* survived more intact than Troy. And it would be a bit obtuse to inquire after the veracity of Tolkien's *Hobbit* and *The Ring.* "We are feeling," says Whitehead, "the actual world with the conscious imputation of imagined predicates, be they true or false" *(ibid.).*

3. *Conscious perceptions.* These, we recall, belong to "a very simplified type of affirmative intuitive judgment." Indeed, there is no absolute difference between them (*PR,* 417). Conscious perception and intuitive judgment together constitute "intellectual feelings," and these intellectual feelings are themselves a division of the feelings called "comparative feelings." The other kind of comparative feelings, a more primitive kind, are called "physical purposes" (*PR,* 406). Whitehead's doctrine of conscious perception is not wholly unequivocal here. In general, however, conscious perception "is the feeling of what is relevant to immediate fact in contrast with its potential irrelevance" (*PR,* 409). Whitehead says that consciousness "flickers," illuminating

brightly only a small area of experience surrounded by a larger "penumbral" area which is insistent but dim (*PR,* 408). The point is that there are degrees of concentration that shade off into more intuitive judgments, which—precisely because they are vague—present less clearly isolated data and claims. This is the domain of causal efficacy. Sharp consciousness glories in the clarity of presentational immediacy. As I write, the page before me is specific in shape, color, location. Less clear, less focused, and carrying me to a solider world beyond than that merely illuminated by attention, is the weight of my body against the chair, the warmth and crackle of a fire a few feet away. Notice that I say the "crackle of the fire." The line between the cause of the perception and the content of the perception is blurred, showing how the causal data come forward when presentational immediacy is not too strongly lit by the focus of conscious attention. Causal data can be submerged and placed all but out of reach by the analysis which conscious perception permits.

The reader should be warned that Whitehead does not here bring together the contrast between the two modes of perception as a means of illustrating the difference between a clean-cut case of conscious perception on the one hand and intuitive judgment on the other. In both cases there is the predication, *in judgment,* of an eternal object as referring to some nexus. Causal efficacy is thus specifically eliminated from pertinence, since the possible proposition that could arise would be of the simple subject-predicate sort, and causal efficacy is polyadic. However, the remarks on "presentational immediacy" as a source of error about "physical feelings" (*PR,* 390) are carried forward to errors in conscious perception as arising from the "integration of the perceptive feeling with this original perceptive feeling" (*PR,* 409). These make it clear that it is proper to refer the continuum between conscious perception and intuitive judgments to the analysis of symbolic reference. And the subject of causal efficacy is reintroduced under the title of the "withness of the body" (*PR,* 474-77), when Whitehead develops the idea of "strain-feelings." These are our spatial and geometrical feelings which issue in their own type of propositional feelings (*PR,* 477). The reader with an appetite for further detail will find that transmutation works over the range of these strain feelings of spatiotemporal "regions" just as it does over the range of quantitative attributions that appear in "intellectual feelings" (*PR*, 478).

For the more normal reader, who may have already discovered a shade more than he wished to know, we return to the three remaining categories of obligation.

III *The Higher Phases of Experience*

The category of Subjective Harmony (viii) is central in the analysis of consciousness. As we have noted, conscious perception is a feeling of a peculiar sort, one which is directed toward the contrast between what is relevant in immediate fact and what is not. This contrast is that between " '*in fact*,' and '*might be*' in respect to particular instances in this actual world." "The subjective form," Whitehead continues, "of the feeling of this contrast is consciousness" (*PR*, 407). This is precisely what he has earlier said about propositional feelings (*PR*, 391). Subjective *form* must be understood in terms of two categories, Subjective Harmony and Subjective Intensity.

1. *Subjective Harmony.* If the scope of the actual occasion be small, its contents simple, and its role in the future not various, this will be because its subjective harmony has been accomplished at the expense of richness of content. If its contents be complex and various, this will be because of the relatively large role played by the category of subjective harmony in the composition of the actual entity. Subjective harmony refers primarily to the rendering compatible of the subjective form of diverse conceptual prehensions (*PR*, 41). Put in dramatic form, the problem of subjective harmony is the problem of drawing contrasts of values away from the pit of mutual elimination or inhibition toward mutual enrichment in a single subjective aim. Whitehead sometimes calls this the "correlation" of subjective forms, or their "mutual sensitivity." All conceptual feelings are feelings of value, we recall. Subjective unity, the first category, deals with purely "logical" situations (*PR*, 389); logical inconsistency means adaptations or elimination of largely factual or physical elements. Subjective Harmony is concerned with "aesthetic adaptations." Diversity can fetch up a real conflict, in simple actual occasions, that is, diversity that does not get beyond the physical. "Unless there is complexity, ideal diversities lead

to physical impossibilities, and thence to impoverishment" (*PR,* 390). Whitehead, in the passages just cited, points out that the self-determination of the actual occasion, in the task of achieving subjective harmony, is "the whole point of moral responsibility." If the freedom of self-making dips into the possibilities of conception and transmutation but little, it is but a little freedom. Conceptual valuation is the awareness of possibility beyond and above the merely physically given. In transmutation this power has already been enormously aggrandized. Yet much of such basic freedom is itself automatic. Sense data are simplifications of the physical world, themselves part of the world process, presenting consciousness with a vast variety of opportunity. So also with the emotional tones which accompany them. The adjustment of possibilities thus revealed is the internal activity called "subjective harmony." Evidently, conceptual harmonization has possibilities for synthesis not given in mere subjective unity.

Human examples, under the circumstances, are hardly misleading. Suppose a man to want peace. He may decide to fight for it, die for it, argue for it, or submit for it. Within each of these decisions, general as each is, he may fight for it by exposing himself to harm, by personal combat, by arousing others, and so on. He may argue for it from the columnist's privileged spot in the newspaper format, as a public speaker, on radio or television, by a novel, an ironic play, a letter to the editors, and so on. And each of these will have its subdivision at still a third level. Again, each of the major decisions has subdivisions that are incompatible with one another; for example, one cannot preserve both anonymity and a personal following in agitating for peace. And there will be cross-categoreal subdivisions that conflict. He cannot decide to fight for peace and argue for it as a nonparticipant. The example is not unduly complex. To be sure, the intent toward peace is an intent not to be realized in a single actual occasion, yet it is in the continuity of just such dominant aims in a series of actual occasions that we recognize a thread of personal order. Singleness of purpose is what defines the reality of the person in question. This fact accounts for the way in which our admiration is aroused by great villains, and not much stirred by our solid citizen neighbor. He has to tie his shoelaces and do even more ignominious things that a Napoleon had done for him.

Where imagination seizes on an objective such as that of peace, all other considerations that can be pertinent must be subordinated and adjusted. This requires conceptual modification of the factually given. Needless to say, there are two risks to be avoided. The first is the tendency to compromise away the aim, in the interest of including many subordinate aims. The second is to see no flexibility in how some particular physical fact embodies a principle, thus identifying a particular physical feeling too closely with too small a range of the conceptual feelings available by means of it. The exact formula can hardly be prescribed in advance. That is, one should not, in logical consistency, expect precise directives for the use of freedom.

2. *Subjective Intensity.* The most appealing metaphor for the problems of subjective harmony is that of levels. We are thus led to the useful conceptions of "perspectives" and "depths." Whitehead makes abundant use of such metaphors, the latter especially in *Religion in the Making* and wherever he assigns a metaphysical role to deity. For example: "Various occasions are thus comparable in respect to their relative depths of actuality" (*RM,* 103). And again, ten pages later, "The essence of depth of actuality—that is of vivid experience—is definiteness." The notion of *Intensity* profits when seen in such a metaphor. Incompatible elements given in a single plane may be rendered compatible on different levels. What is required of the actual occasion is that it be as multiperspectival, as multileveled as possible. But the real point of Intensity lies in its providing *momentum* whereby the aim will carry forward from one actual occasion to the next. The example of the determined seeker for peace is a case of continuity, arising in the context of the problems of subjective harmony.

There isn't a line between categories more difficult to draw than that between subjective harmony and subjective intensity, as they appear in the late phases of the concrescence of an actual occasion. But their emphases are separable. Categories of Obligation, we have seen, are categories of binding, of ligation. The primary task of the category of subjective harmony is an internal unity of adjusted contrasts, through imaginative conceptualization of elements that might otherwise mutually inhibit. Richness and complexity are its achievements. The primary binding is internal. Supervening upon this is the category of subjective intensity which must bring the subjective aim of a single actual occasion into decisive form in what Whitehead calls "physical purposes." This obligation, this binding, is the binding of the actual occasion to its own immediate successors. An enduring object is a complex of chains of order exhibiting similarity in continuity, and novelty and change in growth. Just as surely as the actual occasion is bound by its own self-creation to its matrix-world, so also the constituent serial elements of an enduring object are bound together by more special, more intimate relationships. But it is an essential feature of Whitehead's doctrine (only occasionally qualified) that the primary transmission is physical. There are no merely conceptual differences. Every real difference must make a difference, and its actuality demands that it have its physical side. Whitehead puts this (all too briefly stated) point this way: "The subject aim . . . is intensity of feeling (a) in the im-immediate subject, and (β) in the relevant future" (*PR*, 424). "The greater part of morality hinges on the determination of relevance in the future" (*PR*, 41). He repeats this theme and enlarges it (*PR*, 424 ff.). Needless say, no actual occasion feels the future physically, but in anticipating its own posterity, so to speak, it creates usable potential for that future and in this restricted respect establishes the basis for a bond—the prehension—that the oncoming actual occasion can actualize for itself.

The basis must be physical. In the series of actual occasions which constitute an enduring object "the reverted conceptual feeling is transmitted into the next occasion as physical feeling . . ." (*PR.* 426). Thus conceptual novelties arise which are transmuted into physical experience and are apt for conveyance, or—more strictly—for appropriation in future concretions. These future concretions are mediated by one final category, the ninth, Freedom and Determination.

3. *Freedom and Determination.* This is the category (v. *PR*, 41) which assures that every actual occasion is "internally determined" and "externally free." The language is superficially paradoxical. Whitehead no doubt deliberately chose it to distinguish himself from a familiar view assignable to Kant. (This is more than a guess, but it cannot be defended here. Often, however, a puzzled reader of Whitehead looking for cues or reasons for formulas will profit from guessing that Whitehead is either squeezing the forgotten primary significance out of a word, as in "Obligation," or taking a contrary stance with respect to some familiar formula.) Kant held, speaking popularly, that men are

externally determined and internally free. All of a man's actions, just because they fall into the realm of observation, are—on Kant's view—subject to the iron law of determinism without which observational science is impossible. But an action is rooted in a motive, which motive is not given to observational science, yet is the inward determinant of the act. This doctrine of Kant's is built upon a separation between man as agent and man as object, and further upon a separation between appearances and things-in-themselves. Both of these separations Whitehead rejects. What, then, is the positive meaning of Whitehead's assertion?

The answer, as we have seen, is relatively simple. When an actual occasion is completed, "satisfied," it is completely determined. It perishes and becomes immortal, says Whitehead (e.g., *PR*, 43, 94). Thereby it becomes externally free; that is, a future looms before it in which it can function, *objectively,* as a datum. It is available for an indeterminate number of entities-to-come in an indeterminate number of ways. Its subjectivity is at an end. For this reason its conceptual novelty, its subjective intensity, must have been installed in some physical way (which Whitehead does not explain) that permits its achievement to have significance for future prehending subjects.

IV   *Summary and Renovation*

By now it should be evident that the categoreal obligations are arranged in serial order. The first phase is subjective unity, the last external freedom. A recapitulation of the obligations is thus both a review of the stages, in order, in the concretion of a complex actual occasion, and an opportunity to show the gradual emergence of mind, perception, and consciousness.

The first three categories are not so much phases in the development of an actual occasion as they are the condition for any emergence of any actual occasion. For there to be an actual occasion there must be a primary compatibility among the feelings by which it funds itself and which it has of the antecedent world. Thus, while the feelings are not integrated, they are integrable. This is "Subjective Unity." Moreover, each feeling seizes the world in some uniquivocal way, however complex. No actual occasion "feels" the same objective datum twice.

This condition of self-identity underlies all definiteness including that of logic (*PR*, 39, 344). This is the category of "Objective Identity." Finally there is "Objective Diversity." This means that every felt element in the objective datum maintains its own identity as an element for the actual occasion. No two elements play the same role, just as no two roles (according to Category ii) refer to the same element.

The next three categories refer to the complex middle life of an actual occasion. Here we must think of sufficiently complex cases where these categories are significantly present. It is in these categories that the element of mentality becomes prominent and that elementary feelings proliferate into what amounts to a hierarchy of feelings. It is in this middle life that consciousness is founded.

Category iv is the now familiar category, through and in which the mental pole exhibits its function of prehending eternal objects distinct from their mode of ingression. This is the "derivation" of a conceptual feeling from a physical one. Category iv, "Conceptual Valuation," really only speaks for the possible reproduction of the eternal object in the new actual occasion (*PR*, p. 40). Nothing more is guaranteed. Whitehead's point here is that even conformation of actual occasion to actual occasion, in respect of ingredient eternal objects, involves minimal operation of the mental pole. For the eternal object to be reproduced, however monotonously, it must first be discerned as a distinct entity from its particular appearance in the prior occasion.

It is in Category v, "Conceptual Reversion," that the first glimmers of imagination and significant growth of an organism occur. If one attempts to find where the distinctive features of life—as it is ordinarily but vaguely understood—occur, it is in this category. If "life" be understood as an appropriate term wherever there is self-causation of some sort, then the whole universe is alive and its least units—actual occasions—are also. But if life means "significant and integrated (that is non-disruptive) novelty," then it is in the phase defined by Category v that life emerges. It is through this category, Whitehead tells us, that "novelty enters the world." Novelty is the precondition for freedom; in some ways novelty is nothing more than the evidence of freedom. But it would be equally just to say that the converse is true. And finally, we recall that "life is a bid for feedom."

Conceptual Reversion features a "secondary" conceptual valuation

(*PR,* 380). The first conceptual valuation is the conceptual register of the eternal object given in a physical prehension. This second phase is an awareness of the "proximate novelties"—a sense of other possibilities related to the primarily grasped eternal object. The employment of these secondary alternatives occurs in "Transmutation" (Category vi).

It is in Transmutation that perception in the normal sense occurs. Human perception is complex. It has two modes. The one which enjoys the most evident status is "presentational immediacy." Here perception, "by means of a sensum [ingredient eternal object], rescues from vagueness a contemporary spatial region, in respect to its spatial shape and its spatial perspective from the percipient" (*PR,* 185). As its name indicates, presentational immediacy is concerned with the here-and-now, the transient present, vivid with sense data. But this can hardly cover all perception, in spite of the fact that some philosophers, especially Hume, have tended to treat it so. When we watch Hume reasoning, we find that he wants no part of the dilemma which Santayana calls "the solipsism of the present moment." For one thing, Hume's own doctrine of how we come to rely upon the idea of causation is that copies of our immediate experience are taken in the form of "ideas." From repeated conjunctions among items in our experience which ideation copies we forge (in both senses of "forge"!) the notion of causal necessity. This is really only a "habit" or a custom of so thinking. For Whitehead this is a simple confusion between the "habit of feeling," allegedly causal sequences, and the "feeling of the habit of feeling" such sequences (*PR,* 266). How can the habit be felt if the causes to which it refers cannot be felt? The feeling of the habit is not a feeling of something here-and-now, spatially spread out in technicolor, full sound, and whatever else is sensorily arresting, yet it is no less a feeling. It invokes the sense of time, only minimally present in presentational immediacy, and the sense of *temporal conformity,* which can not be born in one moment of presentational immediacy, nor in any purely externally related series of such moments. To put it in words that Whitehead does not employ, but which are wholly in harmony with his theme, the conformity of the future to the past—which Hume saw no coercive theoretical reason for accepting—is most evident in my own conformation to my own past. Subjectively this conformity is seen in the faculty of memory—which Hume requires in order to give housing to his "habit." Objectively it is given in sheer endurance. If reality is alive and popping at every moment, then "undifferentiated sameness" is not mere qualitative momentum, undeterred by the passage of time, but a new re-creation, in the present, of patterns immediately given in the past. But more than this (which might be argued away or at least eroded by insisting that personal endurance is one thing and objective continuity is another), we do have direct awareness of causal connection at the point of our own experience. *At* the point. Not "in" in the sense that there are certain contents "in" presentational immediacy, but all the same ineradicable. Perception itself is explainable only by invoking bodily awareness. This "withness" of the body (I borrow here from the phenomenologists in order to strengthen Whitehead's point) is not to be confused with the body as perceived. That body is, as the phenomenologists say, a public object, as public as any other. That is the observed body. The "lived body," the felt body, is different. This is the body implicated with consciousness in a way that the most rabid associationist has to admit. Even Hume says we see "with the eyes." This fact, which is given to us directly, is not itself the object of public scrutiny. At best, such scrutiny implies that we see *with* the eye. The *withness* is the body *with* consciousness or—as Whitehead would say—*with* perception. It is not an object of perception. It follows that this mode of perception is distinct from, though interconnected with, presentational immediacy.

Whitehead's name for this other mode is causal efficacy. It is everything that presentational immediacy is not. There are no precise data, no good clean spatial layout, no clear handles on it that let us pick it up and reflect on it. Its entire presence seems to be penumbral to the sharp world of sense. It is vague, felt in temporal extension instead of spatial extension. Slippery, evasive of the clear light of conception, definition, and so on, it has only one thing to be said for it: it is indispensable. A thoroughgoing analysis of its very sibling, presentational immediacy, leads us back to it.

The two modes fuse into symbolic reference. Presentational immediacy is a simplification of the nexūs presented. We do not grasp the individual actual occasions of most nexus; they are given to us not as collections, but under a unification. The wall as a whole is seen characterized by a single eternal object—gray (of some particular shade). Whitehead is willing to have this "gray" be regarded as a secondary quality, "the mediating eternal object being, in this mode of ingression, a secondary quality" (*PR*, 186). But such secondariness does not mean either "illusory" or "less real." It is plain that for Whitehead, the secondariness is a name for the later phase of concretion in which this datum appears. For one thing, neither presentational immediacy nor causal efficacy really advances any claims about what *is*. The one merely presents; the other urges. Error comes in the fusion of the two modes when some proposition felt in some way to be true does not live up to the tests for truth that one may impose.

We are thus driven to consider propositions. Propositions are treated only to the extent of a simple subject-predicate model. There are some brief remarks about metaphysical and logical propositions, but these are fragmentary. Propositions so dealt with are already quite abstract, since the subject-predicate syntax to which they conform is a mirror of the substance-quality view of reality, a view Whitehead does not reject (some popularizations to the contrary, notwithstanding), but which he regards as a simplified abstraction from the world process.

The logical subject of a proposition is a nexus of actual occasions already complete as to their internal, formal constitution. They are—by the ninth category of obligation—already internally determined, but externally free. The prehending subject of the proposition is partial agent in the ingression, which is, say, gray-on-the-wall, as are the objective nexūs themselves. This multirelational occurrence, complex in its origins, has only been skeletonized. Many other factors—which Aristotle would have called "conditions"—must be present also. For example, there must be light, the eye must be healthy, normal, not averted, and so on. "The eye" in turn is but a shorthand for a fantastic complex of actual occasions sequentially occurring as constituents of the one enduring subordinate organism, or—as we would normally say—"organ."

The two modes are fused by the sharing of a common spatial location and ingredient eternal objects. But error, the "price for progress," the risk that accompanies all novelty and freedom, is a chronic possibility. For this reason we invoke testing procedures. For example, the chair behind the mirror cannot be sat upon. Thus the symbol fails to "indicate" as it should. But we must remember that "indication" is itself a complex occurrence arising between self and world. The curious reader may pursue this matter in technical detail for himself (*PR*, 395-405; 411-28; especially 415-16). Whitehead has very little to add to standard analyses of the tactics of confirmation for the claims of propositions. His business is not with such. His role is to frame a metaphysics which (a) does not permit the presuppositions of inductive procedure to be rejected within the system, while being at the same time presumed by the system (e.g., in Hume) and (b) incorporates the manifold character of our experience into one unified—although pluralistic—view. Thus he has warnings for procedural myopia but no far-reaching reforms for inductive method.

Propositions have as their logical subjects nexūs. Hence it is instructive, and only mildly hyperbolic, to say that propositions *are* somewhere. But the other end of a proposition is flapping loose in the winds of possibility. It is a predicate or an eternal object. As proposition the proposition has a predicate that is not necessarily actual. There are true and false propositions. Hence the subject of a proposition must necessarily be actual but not so the predicate.

Propositions are revealed and judged by feelings of a very high order, beginning—at the lower end of the scale—with perceptive feelings. In Whitehead's philosophy the most primitive perception is "feeling the body as functioning" (*PR*, 125). He here means most "primitive" both in the sense that primordial life has this first, as life emerges from non-life, and "primitive" in the sense of "most rudimentary in ourselves." Presentational immediacy is a late acquisition; causal efficacy comes first.

"Conscious perception," on the other hand, "is the most primitive form of judgment" (*PR*, 245). And "only transmuted feelings acquire consciousness" (*PR*, 362). Judgments of perception do not need to be reflectively formed. Indeed, most are not. But they refer to propositions as feeling refers to the felt (*PR*, 293). Judgments are feelings in individual actual occasions, they take up "positions," if you like, about propositions.

We recall that the important part of a proposition is that it be interesting. Truth may add to such interest. Judgments about propositions may be of the "yes" or "no" forms, or they may also be of the "suspended" form. Such suspension may be a reservation of judgment until adequate data can be acquired, as in scientific investigation. Here the proposition, as "theory," is treated as a hypothesis. Or it may be indifferent to truth or falsity, in the literal sense, where imagination has other uses for it. Fables, parables, classroom examples are among such usable functions. So is much of tragedy, as Aristotle observed, when the aim is not history, but the "universal in man."

The line between conscious perceptions and affirmative intuitive judgments is blurred. Such judgments generally are best seen at the point of action. In one direction they fade away—it would seem—into the sense of causal efficacy, the vague awareness of a larger environment. On the other hand they melt into conscious perception and thence to consciousness, which, while it is "flickering" and dependent upon perception, has a vital degree of freedom. If we trace freedom upward from its first phase of sheer creativity, the novelty of the open present moment, it seems to follow the ramifications of mentality. Intuitive perception is guy-wired, anchored to, the given as given, by whatever magical transmutation. Conscious perception, at its conscious end, may be probing hard into the realm of possibility for combinations of eternal objects not immediately actualized in the antecedent members of its nexus nor—conceivably—ever before. As consciousness becomes, in the late phases of a complex actual occasion, more and more dominant, the given is less of a tyrant and more of a challenge. Perception can not, in sanity, stray indefinitely far from the rule of fact.

Categories vii and viii, Subjective Harmony and Subjective Intensity, are peculiarly continuous with one another, as are Reversion and Transmutation. They are the phases in which consciousness reaches its high-water mark. It is in the category of subjective harmony that the task of conciliating contrasting feelings occurs. In this phase contrast, left to its own devices, can produce mutual inhibition. A rigid or monocular view of the possibilities latent in each eternal object, a failure to explore ways of alternatively embodying aims which taken simple-mindedly will clash, results in impoverishment, mutual inhibition. One is reminded here—for we are concerned with eternal objects as possibilities—of the famous dictum that politics is "the art of the possible." The art. There is a suggestion of finesse in the word, in the original sense of "finesse," esthetic discrimination, delicacy. And one is reminded of the powerful tradition of diplomacy of which Whitehead's homeland has long been proud. Consciousness is awareness of the contrast between what might be and what in fact is (*PR,* 409). And Whitehead speaks of the "might be" as the object of "imaginative freedom" (*PR,* 399).

It may seem ludicrous—considering that the life of an actual occasion, even a quite complex one, is no more than a portion of a second—to talk about subjective harmony as an adjustment of aspects of eternal objects which will permit them joint ingression under a common subjective aim. The whole thing sounds too deliberate for the time available. But we recall that each actual occasion is a decision, literally a "cutting off," and that there is nothing to prevent some strands of possibility from being preserved unaltered—through hybrid prehensions which reproduce priorly conceived possibilities *as possibilities*—while others are brought into recognition through conceptual duplication of the physical prehensions by which they become known. The term "moment of decision" neatly reflects the brevity of the time of mutual adjustment, independent of those preparatory moments in which subordinate and contributing decisions supplied the data for more far-reaching and more subtle integrations.

In addition, as Subjective Harmony grades into Subjective Intensity, the relevance of what the future may expect from the present becomes more acute. Here we are in the area of interoccasional, not merely intraoccasional, bonds insofar as any actual occasion can project its own immortality. There is an obvious human lesson to be learned here, commonly ignored, and worth repeating in its metaphysical context: Suppose a man to make decisions where contrasts are removed from potential conflict and subtly synthesized in a way that transcends the sheerly given from which these contracts arise. He does so by a vision of possibility beyond what is normal. In Whitehead's terms, it is the deep penetration into the realm of eternal objects. The scope of such penetration, departing from the temporal and the usual as it does, is broad enough to survive the vicissitudes of much temporal passage. The asymptote approached by such subtlety is everlastingness, and thus what is the common fate of all actual occasions, immortality in the metaphysical sense of unaltering availability, approximates *immortality* in the popular sense of embodying unchanging and significant values.

The last Categoreal Obligation, that of Freedom and Determination, is the end point, the satisfaction of the actual occasion, its "closing up." This is the end of its subjective life and the beginning of its objective future.

CHAPTER 8

Eternal Objects

The last chapter closed on a double note: the subtlety obtained in the realization of value, and the resultant rise toward the survival of value by the transcending of momentary value. This theme sets the stage for a consideration of *eternal* objects. The term "eternity" has—and should have—overtones of a religious sort. Moreover, eternal objects have been described as possible values. In this chapter the emphasis is primarily on eternal objects with little reference to Whitehead's philosophy of religion. In the following chapter the theme of eternal objects and value is continued, with the final emphasis on religion.

I *Eternal Objects, Scale Model*

If Whitehead's account of actual occasions is puzzling, that of eternal objects is adumbrated to the point of exasperation. There is a skeletal but schematic account of them in *Science and the Modern World*. We shall use this as a departure point. Eternal objects are Whitehead's name for what in certain respects have been called "universals." They are "abstract" in the sense that they "transcend particular concrete occasions of actual happening" (*SMW*, 228). But this transcendence does not mean any detachment from temporal actuality of the sort commonly attributed to Plato's forms—at least in the *Republic*. Again we encounter Whitehead's basic premise, the reality of temporality, here in the form of the denial of separate existence to eternal (nontemporal) objects.

An eternal object has an "individual essence" (*SMW*, 229) and a "relational essence" (*SMW*, 230). Its individual essence is its quiddity, its special and distinctive character: loudness (of some particular degree), redness (of some particular shade), and so on. Here we encounter no logical relations, no structure—just brute whatness. In a moment we shall see that this description is best suited to the simplest grade of eternal objects—those of "zero" complexity. Its *relational* essence is twofold: (1) It is internally related to other eternal objects. That is, it has a systematic place in the so-called realm of eternal objects. And though it has a singular identity, it also is (as a "possible") interlocked with other eternal objects, so that it is a member of an indefinitely large number of possible patterns. Since these patterns are mere possible patterns for ingression, they too are eternal objects, of a more complex sort. (2) The relational essence is also present as the eternal object's "patience for such external relations" (*SMW*, 230). How any particular eternal object may be involved in some given actual occasion is determinative, at least partly, for the nature of the actual occasion. An actual occasion is constituted by its feelings of other entities—including eternal objects *qua* objects (as in conceptual prehension). But this actualization, this precipitation, makes no difference to the nature of an eternal object, as such. Indeed, it is somewhat questionable that Whitehead should have used the term "essence" for this peculiarly external relatedness of an eternal object to any actual occasion in which it is ingredient. The justification lies in the fact that while it is irrelevant to the individual essence, or to the internal relatedness among eternal objects, yet it is a vital feature of eternal objects generally that they exist as adjunctive possibilities to the realm of actuality. Whitehead says that an eternal object can not exist "divorced from its reference to other eternal objects, and from its reference to actuality generally; though it is disconnected from its actual modes of ingression into definite [that is, some particular] actual occasions" (*SMW*, 230). He also calls the latter, "the general principle which expresses its ingression in particular actual occasions" (*SMW*, 229).

Eternal objects are arrangeable in strata as to their complexity. The first grade of complexity is called "zero complexity." The easiest examples here are those of color. Whitehead gives us a brief picture of how the complexity of eternal objects relates them to one another (*SMW*, 237-41). Consider three colors, *A, B, C.* Each of these belongs to the "zero" level. There will then be another eternal object *R*, of the first level of complexity, relating the three colors in some definite way to one another. Call this *"R (A, B, C)."* Let it be the three colors oriented to one another in a specific way on three of the four faces of a tetrahedron. Here we have a case of a "relational essence." "This relational essence is determinable by reference to that object alone, and does not require reference to any other objects, except those which are specifically involved in its individual essence when that essence is complex . . ." (*SMW*, 236-37). If we put another quotation alongside the first, we are in a position to draw some conclusions: "the relational essence of an eternal object is not unique to that object" (*SMW*, 237).

What is meant by this last remark? The relational essence of an eternal object may apply elsewhere. Easy enough. *R* of *A, B, C* allows us to change *A, B, C* colors for others, without *R's* being altered. Let *A, B, C* be red, green, purple, instead of blue, orange, yellow. Or let only one change. The zero complexity terms would remain of the same type—colors—but *that relation* could hold among *other* colors. However, what of the relational essence of the zero complexity eternal objects? *All* eternal objects have a twofold relational essence. By definition, they cannot be analyzed into subordinate internally related terms. Here again, an answer seems clear. Their internal relatedness—that is, their relational essence, so far as it refers exclusively to the realm of eternal objects and not to some particular actual occasion—must be of the reciprocal sort: that they *can* function in more complex eternal objects, but that they share this *can* (possibility, which is the common character of all eternal objects) with others. Their relational essence is not unique to them. Thus eternal objects are "isolated, because their relationships as possibilities are expressible without reference to their respective individual essences" (*SMW*, 238). This means then that the claim that the "relational essence is determinable by reference to that object alone, and does not require reference to any other objects" must be interpreted as meaning "to any other *particular* eternal objects," in the case of simple (zero-grade) eternal objects. It cannot mean that the relational essence of a simple object *A*, which has no subordinate structure like that of *R (A, B, C)* is deducible from its individual essence.

As to the internal relations among objects, this is as far as we can profitably go with *Science and the Modern World.* In the schematic of *Science and the Modern World,* only colors and shapes are given as examples of eternal objects. This is done for the sake of simplicity. But several questions arise. Are the only eternal objects of zero complexity colors? Are mathematical eternal objects like the tetrahedron in the example always of complexity one or higher? Most important of all, is there a general definition of an eternal object? This last question has a definite answer, but it does not appear in *Science and the Modern World.* What about generic terms for qualities such as "color," "shape," and so on? Are these terms for eternal objects? If so, what happens when red ingresses, does color ingress too? Surely the answer is yes. Is this, then, the ingression of one eternal object or two? A partial answer is given in *Process and Reality,* but not a complete one. These and related questions will be dealt with shortly, but two further matters need to be explained first.

(1) Eternal objects are abstract. Simple eternal objects are possible components of more complex ones. In every actual occasion there is a limited number of eternal objects actualized. They are related in one complex ingression. These ingredient eternal objects can be arranged according to a scale of increasing complexity, the members of the higher levels having those of lower levels as components. As we rise up these levels of complexity, the more complex eternal objects will become less numerous. At the highest level of complexity there will be a single complex eternal object, at the "vertex" of a "finite hierarchy" of eternal objects (*SMW*, 243). Its members will be all the subordinate eternal objects in just the relations in which they are found in the actual occasion. The summit eternal object is thus the entire skeleton of the actual occasion, but void of spatiotemporality, the primary condition of actuality. Such an eternal object is obviously more concrete than any of its subordinate components, since it is closer to telling the full story about the actual occasion—or the nexus. "Red" is a very abstract designation applying to a great range of entities; "red book" is less so over a smaller range. "Thick red book" further specifies limits and comes closer to particularity and actuality. Individuals have often been treated, in the history of philosophy, as intersects of complex universals, for this reason. And with some cause. But to do so is to ignore the spatiotemporal conditions of true singularity—that of an

actual occasion. The fallacy committed is one of abstraction. We see a double meaning for "abstraction." The complex eternal object at the vertex of a finite hierarchy is not very abstract from what is actual (*SMW*, 246). For example, we send photographs to our friends, saying, "These are our children now." Or we look at the detailed relief model of a mountain range and say, "There's the mountain we climbed." Where simpler eternal objects are employed, common sense steps in and acknowledges the abstraction. Of a quick effort we say, "This is a sketch *of* our house," or of a fleeting isolation of a datum, "That's the color *of* Mary Ellen's car." These commonplace usages embody a lesson. The lesson is not to trust an account of perception which begins with the most abstract data imaginable, namely minimal sense data of little or no complexity, and undertakes to give a concrete picture of perception by merely synthesizing these data. Vital relations may have been lost by starting with these *disjecta membra*. This procedure Whitehead calls "sensationalism." He repeatedly shows its bankruptcy and how it thwarts or distorts the vision of, for example, Locke and Hume (*PR*, 221-23). Sensationalism is another example of "The Fallacy of Misplaced Conreteness."

(2) One other basic problem is discussed in *Science and the Modern World* with regard to eternal objects. This problem will be somewhat simpler for our having considered Whitehead's views of mentality in *Process and Reality*. The world is a processive and therefore incomplete actuality. But at any given moment, we should on principle, by a web of prehensions, be able to trace our way from any actual occasion, *a*, to any other, *b*. Epistemologically this world seems to require that we know everything before we know anything. Thoroughgoing investigation of the flower in the crannied wall should unravel the mysteries of super-novae. This problem worried the idealists a great deal, since like Whitehead they were committed to powerful doctrines of internal relations. The sensationalists, logical atomists, and related breeds with strong skeptical commitments to doctrines of *external* relations, have few or no problems of the sort. Rather, their problem is how one knows anything at all.

Old-fashioned as it is, the problem is hardly dispensable, since it bears on the question of truth. Whitehead's position here begins by admitting "that it is impossible to complete the description of an actual occasion by means of concepts" (*SMW*, 245). The word "concept" directs our attention to the role of mentality. Restrospectively we can see the relation between conceptual prehension and eternal objects beginning to emerge in Whitehead's thought. The same is true for the doctrine of Symbolic Reference. The "connectedness of an actual occasion" entails that there be an associated "infinite abstractive hierarchy." The "finite abstractive hierarchy" is but a segment of the infinite hierarchy. What is the relation and distinction between the two? The answer is that there is a "hierarchy of concepts" applicable to the eternal objects of the infinite hierarchy, but only a selection of them is actually seized upon in the perspective of any new actual occasion (*SMW*, 245-47). This "abruptness," as Whitehead calls it, means that

the things apprehended as mental are always subject to the condition that we come to a stop when we attempt to explore ever higher grades of complexity in their realised relationships. We always find that we have thought of just this—whatever it may be—and of no more. There is a limitation which breaks off the finite concept from the higher grades of illimitable complexity. (*SMW*, 247)

The language here is the language of a limited mental penetration of the given, a finite conceptual grasp (either in Whitehead's technical meaning for "conception" or the popular one) of the encountered world. Every actual occasion is finite in time; it is in fact quite brief. The processes of self-composition in an actual entity define the limits of its finite hierarchy of eternal objects. Again, in *Process and Reality*, Whitehead says, "But 'decision' cannot be construed as a casual adjunct of an actual entity. It constitutes the very meaning of actuality" (*PR*, 68).

The "eternal objects" of *Science and the Modern World* are limited models. Shapes and colors carry the burden of example.

II   *Eternal Objects as a Realm*

The ruling definition of eternal objects in *Process and Reality* is permissive to the point of introducing more than any study can handle clearly. Whitehead says, "Any entity whose conceptual recognition does not involve a necessary reference to any definite actual entities of

the temporal world is called an 'eternal object' " (*PR*, 70). This is an
echo of his early definition of objects as whatever can "be again" (*CN*,
144). Not much is written about this sentence, even when it is
mentioned, and we sympathize. Yet when a professional logician says
"any" we should listen and think.

To begin with, what does the definition not say? (1) It does not
identify a separate realm of eternal objects, of the sort that Plato's
forms seem to be in the *Republic*. (2) It does not have anything to do
with perfection, or the good, or what-have-you. It is true that
Whitehead, in a preceding passage, speaks of the "Platonic forms," but
the context is one in which he is speaking of a characteristic of Plato's
forms which they share with eternal objects: the fact that the total
multiplicity of them is not "given." And, in his last work, Whitehead
explicitly detaches himself from not only the neo-Platonic tradition,
but the Plato of the *Parmenides*. Of the idea of perfection he says it is
"naive" to attach it to the realm of forms. How about "the forms of
evil, and other forms of imperfection?" (*MT*, 94). (3) It says nothing at
all about any agency arising from eternal objects. As sheer possibility,
they wait upon precipitating occasions to actualize them. To be sure
Whitehead frequently speaks of the "ingression" of eternal objects, and
even says that they "ingress into" actual occasions. But these are modes
of speech. The formal doctrine is that of the Eighteenth Category of
Explanation, called the "ontological principle." It states, in brief, that
"actual entities are the only *reasons;* so that to search for a *reason* is to
search for one or more actual entities" (*PR*, 37).

What the definition does say raises many questions, however.

Consider the problem mentioned in the preceding section: Are the
mathematical eternal objects always of some degree of complexity
greater than zero? If we ask, as a prefatory question, "Is the eternal
object, the tetrahedronality, 'composed' of subordinate eternal objects
that are triangles?" the answer would seem to be "yes," from the cues
Whitehead gives us. There should be an *R (S, T, V)* similar to the *R (A,
B, C)* of *Science and the Modern World* where the variables are triangles
instead of colors. But many problems arise. For one thing, *S, T,* and *V,*
apart from some particular ingression, are the *same* equilateral
triangle—assuming that the tetrahedron is regular. Let us pass over that
difficulty and take it that the equilateral triangle is of lesser

complexity. However, *R (A, B, C)* was said to be of the "lowest complex grade" *(SMW,* 240), that is, grade 1. Then, either (a) *R (S, T, V)* is of a higher complex grade than *R (A, B, C)* or (b) *S, T,* and *V* are eternal objects of grade 0, together with *A, B,* and *C.* We should then have a negative answer to the first question in this paragraph. This conclusion is reinforced by the fact that (a) seems unacceptable, since it would mean that the sheer characteristic of tetrahedronality was of greater complexity—and thus closer to the concrete—than tetrahedronality with three of its four surfaces specified as to color. But this is contrary to Whitehead's doctrine of abstraction, which we examined above. However, (b) also seems unacceptable, for if *S, T,* and *V* (or the one equilateral triangle that is "used" four times over; it makes no difference here) are of the same (zero) grade of complexity, they (or it) can not be further analyzed. But this erects a barrier between a triangle and what we normally think of as its "components": line segments.

We promptly run into a tangle of questions here which only very technical analysis can illuminate, let alone solve. The present difficulty can be given a provisional solution. Whitehead was well aware of the question of how geometrical entities are related to actuality. In his early works he devises a set of tactics for deriving geometrical entities from our common experience.[1] This procedure, called "The Method of Extensive Abstraction," is revised and renovated in *Process and Reality,* there appearing as the "Method of Extensive Connection." At the point where Whitehead undertakes to give some fecund meaning to Euclid's use of the notion of "evenness" (undefined in Euclid), while showing that certain geometrical properties can be found in the continuum, "without any recourse to measurement," Whitehead defines a tetrahedron. He does so in terms of four noncoplanar points. A triangle is defined in terms of three noncolinear points *(PR,* 467, 466). He thus bypasses the mediation between tetrahedrons and points by "constituent" triangles and lines.

This will have to serve as showing how the levels of complexity might be handled so as to avoid dilemmas of the sort considered above. It still leaves open the question of the status of these other geometrical entities with respect to one another, however, in the realm of eternal objects. That question too must be referred to a general warning, rather than getting a precise solution. I state the warning as follows: the levels of abstraction discerned in any one hierarchy are not necessarily the same as those in another hierarchy and thus do not necessarily belong to the same scheme of stratification, even when the same eternal object appears in the two hierarchies. In terms of a visual model, this means that one could not necessarily put two hierarchies diagrammatically on a blackboard (without superimposition), even if the same eternal object is an item in each hierarchy.

The foregoing example likely does not arouse the intellectual passion of all readers. But for anyone who wishes to understand eternal objects beyond seeing them as repeatables in nature, it serves at least as an introduction to several themes.

(1) The conclusion to be drawn from the example is that the modes of relations between eternal objects are themselves multifarious. The boundlessness of the realm of eternal objects extends not merely to the zero-level membership, then, but to the possible combinations as well, and hence to types of abstraction (cf. *SMW*, 243).

(2) Numbers as well as shapes, unsurprisingly, have status as mathematical forms (*AI*, 322). Judging from the elaborate efforts of *Principia Mathematica* in the definition of the number "one," we may surmise that at least that number and the geometrical conception of a point constitute mathematical objects of zero complexity. Through-out his writings, Whitehead preserves the distinction between these idealized mathematical notions and their tempting experiential analogues. For example, he makes a sharp distinction between the number "one" and the subcategory "one," which together with "creativity" and "many" comprise the "Category of the Ultimate" (*PR*, 31). He gives semantic, rather than mathematical, examples for what is designated by "one."

(3) Generalizing the theme in (1), although eternal objects collectively are repeatedly said to be a "realm" (*SMW*, Chapter 10), that realm has (a) no single unifying principle, (b) no all-inclusive apical eternal object including all others as constituents, nor (c) any group of such apices (one for each mode of abstraction). It has (d) no stratification toward an ultimate ideal, like Plato's *agathon* (we have seen already that there are forms of imperfection), and (e) it has no preferential orders which confer greater or less reality on actualities

that embody entities from it. The exasperated critic might well say, "Some realm."

Whitehead indeed tends to shy away from the term "realm" after *Science and the Modern World*. In *Process and Reality* he calls it a "multiplicity" (46), indicating the looseness, or better the democracy among orders of eternal objects, and echoes the theme elsewhere (*PR*, 69). He repeats this designation again shortly and warns us that there is no one entity which is the *class* of all eternal objects. A multiplicity, he says, "has no unity derivative *merely* from its various components" (*PR*, 73).

A realm without a ruler. An unbounded collection incapable of being collected. These are only partially correct caricatures. We shall see that there is a kind of ruler, God, in his Primordial Nature, and a kind of unity.

(4) The unity of a multiplicity is largely a negative one as far as existence goes. In the context of exposing the role of God in the world process Whitehead says, "Thus the many eternal objects conceived in their bare isolated multiplicity lack any existent character" (*PR*, 530). We recall that unity is primarily what happens in actualization, in the *unifying* of prehensions in an actual occasion. As to *logical* unity, we have seen that there are logical restrictions, but no *one* logical order. If we call eternal objects "non-existent intelligibles apt for realization in existence," we have touched enough high points. "Non-existent" is a character for each of them, but a distillation of this negative character does not afford a unifying character, rather a characteristic to be understood in terms of another realm: actuality. "Intelligibility" again is a relational characteristic, requiring reference to some actual mentality, that is, something which is *not* an eternal object. And "aptitude for actualization" also is meaningful only in terms of the existent. Moreover, of multiplicities in general, which are classified as one of the eight categories of existence (*PR*, 32-33), Whitehead says they are not "proper entities" really, since a "multiplicity has solely a disjunctive [hence a negative] relationship to the actual world." Effort to treat its unity as one would that of a proper entity, consequently, "produces logical errors" (*PR*, 44-45), perhaps just such difficulties as those arising from the consideration of geometrical objects. Or such difficulties as might arise from asking if the ingression of red is the

ingression of one eternal object or two, since red is an "instance" of a "general principle"—in this case "color," which is also an eternal object, presumably of a higher grade of complexity (*PR*, 295-96).

If we accept this presentation of eternal objects we may not see how to get out of such troubles, but we do see why to *stay* out of them. However, it must be remembered that we have been discussing multiplicities, not eternal objects. The realm of eternal objects is a multiplicity, and while incautious questions about the internal structure of that realm may lead to logical confusion, there is nothing *outré* about eternal objects themselves. They are of the common stuff of our experience. Indeed, the fifth category of existence is "Eternal Objects"—merely as a category, not as a subgroup of "Multiplicities"—and Whitehead says of the first category, "Actual Entities," and the fifth, "Eternal Objects," that they "stand out with a certain extreme finality" (*PR*, 33).

III   *Eternal Objects as a Category*

Do eternal objects collectively, then, have no structure to exhibit that can be probed by logical expertise? In his last public lecture Whitehead says that the "variation in the grades of ideas is endless."[2] So the task of analysis must be endless. But it does have a beginning. There is a major division of the realm of eternal objects. Eternal objects are either of the "objective species" or of the "subjective species."

We recall that the two modes of perception which unite to give Symbolic Reference share two characteristics, *location* and the *sense datum* itself. The former of these has to do with "objective" eternal objects, the latter with "subjective" ones.

(1) Objective eternal objects. These are the "mathematical platonic forms. They concern the world as a medium" (*PR*, 446). We have already some acquaintance with these. They include both shape and number. Their primary function is that the objective "solidarity of the world" rests upon them (*ibid*.).

It is easy to abandon this solidarity as simply meaning reliably "there," as opposed to the "subjective" eternal objects to be discussed shortly. But we already know that we must not smuggle any distinctions in that will divide up the world into separate realities.

Moreover, it is quite as easy to be wrong about shapes and numbers as it is about, say, colors. We should not try to fit "objective" and "subjective" into the classical "primary" and "secondary" distinction.

Objectivity apparently is to be understood in a relational context alone. Objectivity is the absence of subjectivity. In Whitehead's vocabulary an eternal object of the objective species, considered simply in itself, "can dictate no subjective form for its prehension. But green [an eternal object of the subjective species] can. And there lies the difference between the sensa and the abstract mathematical forms" (*AI*, 322). We note in passing that primary features of any definition of subjectivity will have to omit any direct reference to "objectivity," on pain of a charge of circularity.

Pre-Kantian empiricism tended to regard objectivity as governed by reliability and susceptibility to mathematical ordering. Kant treats objectivity as what stands over against one's will. Whitehead defines it as that which in itself carries no emotive or affective tone. It invokes no subjective involvement. Like all eternal objects, the mathematical ones are values—but not much more than logical values. Subjectivity is the sign of an upward groping toward esthetic value, as apart from the factual transfer of physical value. One subordinate reason, closely allied to the above, is that lower organisms, including those that might not pass for organisms at all (in ordinary parlance) share the condition of objectivity with the higher ones.

(2) Subjective eternal objects. We can throw some light on the two kinds of eternal objects by considering the ways in which eternal objects can ingress. We recall that basically any eternal object ingresses polyadically. In the minimum case of perception of a quality, for instance, the eternal object "orange" ingresses with a "mode of location" "over there," but with its bodily conditions for being known over here. To be, for perception, is to be perceived in a multiple relation. Substances merely qualified by properties are abstractions from events multiply related.

There are three fundamental modes of ingression. There is (1) ingression as datum, (2) ingression as "an element in the definiteness of the subjective form of some feeling"; or (3) ingression as the datum of "a conceptual, or propositional, feeling" (*PR*, 445). All other modes are then said to be interpretations of these basic ones.

Whitehead continues by making the distinction between objective and subjective eternal objects rest on this trichotomy: Objective eternal objects do not have the second mode of ingression available. Subjective form is not for them.[3]

As an example of this distinction, we are given the following: "Our developed consciousness fastens on the sensum as datum: our basic animal experience entertains it as a type of subjective feeling. The experience starts as that smelly feeling, and is developed by mentality into the feeling of that smell" (*AI,* 315). Such localizations begin primarily as a sense-awareness—which Whitehead believes is never a matter of indifference—and then take on an isolable and associable character, clarifying themselves as data, not as mere feelings. "The steady values," he says, "derived from sense-perception, which are there even when disregarded and even when jarring with other emotions, exist because the sensa themselves enter into the subjective forms of their physical prehensions" (*AI,* 322).

There seem to be three considerations here. (1) We often ignore the fact that there is a time lapse between the vague awareness of a qualitative datum and the clarification of its spatial features, locale, size, shape, and so on. The lapse is rather brief in the case of optical data, but discernible with attention. Whitehead points out that there are moods which even function as substitutes for sensa, directly grasped, in babies and animals where the intellective operations are slight: sensed anger, joy, and so on (*AI,* 315-16). These psychological facts might be quarreled with or even interpreted away; but we find them in something close to "immediate experience." Whatever else these examples show, they amplify the body's primary "withness" as essential to ingression. But this withness is required for all ingressions. (2) There is as well, what has been mentioned before, the recognition that the roots of complex values must extend into primitive and elementary value experience as their foundation. But this leaves open the question of why the mathematical forms are, so to speak, emotional blanks. Whitehead clearly does not mean to indicate that we take no joy in elegant mathematical proofs, that the figure of a star has no appeal, or that tessellations do not interest us. But I think he would have to appeal to cultural, personal, and other such factors to account for our "subjective evaluations" in these cases. A more pressing example would be the swastika, which still is *non grata* (even if it be the counterclockwise symbol of the Southwestern Indians). This brings us to the third consideration. (3) The point about these "objective" eternal objects is that they exhibit properties of severe logical rigor. These are their essential characteristics which remain for examination, after we have removed the warm flesh of emotional feeling. We do not value these relations up or down; our creative powers are limited to unmasking their kinship system. We cannot alter them. This is the root meaning of the "solidarity of the world." In this respect, Whitehead has come by two routes, and obliquely, to Kantian considerations. The "objective" eternal objects stand over against my will and thereby exhibit their inflexible "objectivity." And secondly Whitehead is asking in his own way, "How is mathematics possible?" just as Kant did. Whitehead is quite overt on this point: We recall that an actual occasion can be divided "genetically" or "coordinately." Dividing it genetically, we analyze its prehensions and what they relate to. Coordinately, we analyze its extensity, its spatiotemporal aspects. As Whitehead says, "Thus the coordinate division of an actual entity produces feelings whose subjective forms are partially eliminated and partially inexplicable" (*PR,* 447). What is probably meant here is that the "higher phases" are dropped out (eliminated) and the primitive sense objects of zero complexity, being unanalyzable, become irrelevant. Irrelevant to what? To measurement and the theory of extensive connection required for measurement. Two pages after the above quotation Whitehead launches this subject, in the context of "extensive connection." The technical discussion of the realm of objective eternal objects is of "points, lines, and surfaces, and of straightness and flatness." This is the domain of the objective immortality of actual occasions, beyond their subjective phases. In this domain final cause is no longer germane. The atomicity of occasions is exchanged for the continuum of extension, and the ruling considerations of "cause" for those of efficient causation (*PR,* 448). In short, this is the heartland of observational science.

Most of what we should normally call "values" arise in the realm of the subjective form and hence among the ingressions of eternal objects of the subjective species, which alone may enter the actual occasion in this way.

But we must not suppose that, if the "solidarity" of the world rests on the continuities of extension and the ingredient "objective" eternal objects therein, there is some primacy about the ingression of such objects in the world process. Indeed, even in our own sophisticated experience, the first rush of awareness is emotional, however tame, controlled, or familiar. In this case (and it is not always so) what *comes* first *is* first. "The primitive form of physical experience is emotional—blind emotion—received as felt elsewhere in another occasion and conformally appropriated as a subjective passion" (*PR*, 246). We are so used to dealing with factual attitudes toward sensory data—for example, the stove as being green—that we forget this emotional primacy. "Yet, the aesthetic feelings, whereby there is pictorial art, are nothing else than products of the contrasts latent in a variety of colours qualifying emotion . . ." (*PR*, 246-47). "Thus the primitive experience is emotional feelings ["feeling" in the English edition], felt in its relevance to a world beyond" (*PR*, 247). We are reminded here of the mode of causal efficacy, the vaguer, deeper mode of "perception" which functions throughout nature, giving us a sense of a spatial and temporal "beyond" not found in presentational immediacy. Actual occasions do not necessarily enjoy the same kinds of primitive emotions. As "green" functions for a person in the act of esthetic synthesis and enjoyment, so "pulses of emotion" show up in elementary particles as wavelengths and vibrations, according to Whitehead, repeated successively as "primitive feeling" from actual occasion to actual occasion *(ibid.)*. This theme is repeated: "The intensity of physical energy belongs to the subjective species of eternal objects, but the peculiar form of the flux of energy belongs to the objective species" (*PR*, 447). The shape, the frequency, the amplitude, the number of the pulses of energy, these are matters of measurement and extension. But the integrity, the sheer vitality—the *"in*tensity" (as opposed to the *ex*tensity), that is the evidence of the subjective element, conforming to its ancestors. Thus, "conformation" is the same as "reproduction" or "re-enaction" (*PR*, 364).

The conclusion to all this is clear: *every deviation from total conformation is evidence of the creative element of mentality at work.* But this is not "creativity" in the necessarily constructive sense of the word. It might be better to use the more neutral term "novelty." The man who sees the foreign spies materializing through the plate glass window is close to a destruction of his integral personality. All the same, this is evidence of the mental failing in its task of producing coherent adventures among eternal objects, suggested by the "given" ones. Without reference to such "coherence," "harmony," "depth of feeling," and so on, we find a metaphysical indifference to the destructive and constructive aspects of novel origination. Eternal objects as subjective invoke the question of value.

CHAPTER 9

Value and Valuation

I *Emotion*

Whitehead has—once more—stretched a term beyond its normal meaning in order to have it cover those faint stirrings and suggestions from which the more sophisticated and complex instances arise. The term is "emotion." We should not ignore the advantages gained by rendering normal modes of speech and thought intelligible thereby. Consider two emotions: rage and contentment. Both of these are emotions in the normal sense. On Whitehead's view they are complex transformations into a series of closely coordinated (human) actual occasions, arising from more deep-laid continuities of emotion private to subordinate actual occasions and societies, and therefore not directly data of consciousness at all. Yet we can, through technological cleverness, expose these relations. In the case of rage, for example, its emotional content, as a *sheer datum,* can be given by an injection of adrenalin. The same holds true of contentment. Oral drugs and brain electrode intrusions will produce contented feelings. We are tempted to leap to the conclusion that the reality of rage is thus "purely" physical. For one thing, the physical interpretation loses something of its narrowness and its repulsiveness if we extend the notions of mentality and emotionality all the way down the scale of being, from the human to the electronic. One should not then be shocked or disillusioned to find that "mental" states are in intimate association with "physical" states. He is reminded that either "state" conceived as belonging to a self-sufficient domain of the "purely physical" or the "purely mental" is inadequate to account for rather unavoidable facts. Felt emotion can arise from electrical and chemical stimulus. Few of us look with unblinking enthusiasm upon the fact that a sense of pleasure or contentment can be induced by inserting electroconductive wires into the human brain. It might be useful to attempt a Whiteheadian approach to this fact:

The fact that we can engender emotional states by chemical or electrical tampering demonstrates the intercommitment of the mental and physical aspects of process. However, the tendency to identify the nonphysical element here as reducible, without loss, to the physical ignores at least two facts.

(1) The actuality of the emotion is as real as that of the stimulus but qualitatively distinct from it. (a) An analogous warning applies to efforts to "identify" the blue of an early Picasso with its associated wavelength, namely, there is a confusion of two quite distinct *types of emotion* (in Whitehead's sense of "emotion"), having different consequences and belonging to different strata of abstraction. (b) Further, it ignores the fact that such blue may be vividly recalled in waking retrospect or in a dream without the wave disturbance of normal perception. There are people, for example, who have absolute pitch in colors and can match memory to fact. (c) Moreover, minute variations in wave frequency "produce" no discernible difference in color sensitivity. To introduce the idea of thresholds here—for example, that of the "Just Noticeable Difference"—is helpful clinically, but far from eliminating the independence of the "subjective" aspects of color sensitivity, it underscores it. (d) Perception is bodily; it occurs from within the world, not from beyond it. The data of perception thus stand on an equal footing if only because they are the basis of all inference, scientific, esthetic, sociological, and so on.

(2) The identification of the emotion as "rage" or "contentment" places it under the same label as other such states. This abstract grouping is the result of a misunderstanding of the mode of perception called "presentational immediacy." If we fasten on the abstracted emotion now, under adrenalin injection, we cannot identify it with that which is aroused, for example, by pictures of human suffering on innocent faces caught in the crush of a meaningless war. Rage, concretely, is rage *at;* contentment is contentment *about.* There is a vector quality about emotions that carries them beyond the immediacy of the moment. This "beyond" is a temporal beyond. It invokes what

Whitehead has called "causal efficacy." Such causal efficacy is not infallible, as Hume showed and as Kant agreed. That is not the point; the point is that it will not be satisfied unless some temporal relation is given which completes our understanding of the here and now. We cannot settle for the given emotion here and now as concrete. There is the nagging sense of incompletion. The very assigning of anger to the adrenalin shot is the satisfaction of this demand, not its rejection. Whitehead's view differs from the scientistic one in insisting that the causal relationship is internal, constitutive of the identity of the datum as much as any qualitative vividness of it may be. Rage-at-war and rage-from-adrenalin are the same only at a remote level of focus on the present extremely upset feeling. One feeling is representative of the continuity of a person with conscious reasons extending backward through the continuity of a life. The other depends upon a bodily continuity only, and personality is not among the constituents of an observable body. The distinction just drawn is not impractical or theoretical. For example, the degree to which vector qualities are lacking in pathological emotions is doubly significant in psychological diagnosis. First, if vector pointers are missing after sufficient investigation, then the question of hormonic or related bodily imbalance arises. Second, if there is then a failure to discover *physical* reasons as well, then the psycho-diagnostician is helped in estimating the depth and nature of the emotional disturbance. And on this he bases his estimate of the time and extent of therapy. Thus is the term "un-conscious" justified.

II   *Values*

Before *Process and Reality* Whitehead's emphasis is on *values*. In *Process and Reality* and afterward it is on *valuation*. The *works* thus made their impression on their own author: the *process*, "valuation," becomes the dominant theme. However, the doctrine itself—under whatever name—with a few problems of vocabulary, can be coherently exhibited for all but highly technical purposes.

"Value," we have repeatedly recalled, Whitehead calls "the word I use for the intrinsic reality of an event" (*SMW,* 136). The immediately preceding passage says:

Remembering the poetic rendering of our concrete exprience, we see at once that the element of value, of being valuable, of having value, of being an end in itself, of being something which is for its own sake, must not be omitted in any account of an event as the most concrete actual something. *(Ibid.)*

And directly following these remarks Whitehead resolves to "transfer" to the very texture of realization itself the value which we recognize so readily in terms of human life. The theme is picked up and explained in *Religion in the Making.* Whitehead's point is interlocked with a number of others: The reality of time means a real creativity, otherwise the *novelty* of time is illusory. But this creativity issues in atomic actual occasions. They exhibit order among themselves, and within themselves. They are self-creating but not *ex nihilo;* they make themselves as new beings from the data provided by the old beings. The doctrine of time includes the notion of the openness of the present and the closedness of the past. The fixity of the past is strong and inflexible. It constitutes an immediate limitation on what the present creativity can accomplish. The parts of *Science and the Modern World* that we have just been considering deal with this condition of affairs under the title of "limitation." To identify these "limitations" is a far cry from holding that the past is *active* in the present. The past, if closed, has lost all direct agency. It will be heard from, in that its definiteness sets bounds to how it can be used. But this is not agency. If agency is in the present and order emerges—either the repetitive order of sheer endurance or the generative order which is commonplace in growth and evolution of all sorts—then it must be that some end is sought for, some "striving" is present. However, striving is relational; we do not merely strive, we "strive for." Value is the generic term for what is striven for. The first phase of striving is merely to be.

The unit value is the *actualized* occasion. I use the term "actualized" to stress the nongeneric character of value. "There is," says Whitehead, "no such thing as bare value. There is always a *specific* value, which is the created *unit* of feeling arising out of the specific mode of concretion of the diverse elements (*RM,* 103; italics mine). An event, in *Science and the Modern World,* is said to be a "matter of fact" that is a "value for itself," that requires, nonetheless, the rest of the universe in order to come into existence (*SMW,* 278). The nonexistence of bare value thus means: (1) there is no "form" of value, with realities arrangeable on a scale of conformity to the ideal; (2) hence value is always actual, not abstract; (3) there is, equally, no isolation of value, since the self-valuing creature draws its values, at least in the primitive phases, from the antecedent world.

(4) The nonexistence of "bare value" means one more thing: value is not a quality in the conventional sense, or a property, nor is it an analyzable goal; value refers to order, achieved order: "There is an actual world because there is an order in nature. If there were no order, there would be no world" (*RM,* 104). Berkeley held that to be was to be perceived. This doctrine is absorbed as a partial truth in Whitehead's doctrine of objective existence: for Whitehead, to come into existence is to value; to exist is to be valued. But we are concerned here with the initial phase of subjectivity in the self-creative process of an actual entity. At this stage, to be is to perceive (read "prehend") and to order what is so prehended from this subjective viewpoint: to synthesize, integrate.

There are two immediate points to be noticed here. (1) All eternal objects are supposed to be possible values. Eternal objects of the objective species, geometrical and mathematical elements, concern nature as a continuum, in neglect of her atomicity, and therefore in neglect of her qualitative features. The scene is stripped to extensity, if these objects alone be considered. We see why they qualify as eternal objects, since they provide a matrix for a dominant type of order—the extensive continuum. We also see why they are said, these "objective" objects, to have no ingress into the subjective forms of actual occasions. The objective/subjective contrariety suggests this, of course, but cannot itself be appealed to, on pain of circularity. What is wanted- is justification for the use of the dichotomy—and it consists in just this: the mathematical order of the continuum is indifferently the same *qua* pure *extensity,* inflexible, *unmodifiable* (again the quasi-Kantian conception of intransigence before will), like justice—blind and the same for all. Eternal objects of the subjective species are susceptible of *intensity,*with supple valuations "up" and "down" open to the actual occasion. Thus are the two notions of "intensity" and "order" intercommitted with respect to "value." According to the freedom, and the fixity as well, of its inheritance, an actual occasion determines the intensities of its constituents. This is but another way of viewing its self-creation—that it *is* how it becomes. "The zero of intensiveness means the collapse of actuality.... Various occasions are thus comparable in respect to their relative depths of actuality" (*RM*, 103). (2) The other point is that Whitehead is completely rejecting any neo-Platonic theory of negative value. Negative value is not mere defect of being. It may be narrowness of achieved value, or elimination of values through mutual inhibition (which is conflict of being, not want of it), or bad timing, but good and evil originate alike as achieved values:

> Evil, triumphant in its enjoyment, is so far good in itself; but beyond itself it is evil in its character of a destructive agent among things greater than itself.... Evil is positive and destructive; what is good is positive and creative.... There is evil when things are at cross purposes. (*RM*, 95-97; cf. *PR*, 517)

"Insistence on birth at the wrong season is the trick of evil" (*PR*, 341).

What terms should be used to refer to value, in general? Should they be religious, esthetic, moral, social? The answer is esthetic. The answer is deliberate, calculated. The primacy of esthetic language, for Whitehead, rests on the primacy of esthetic value.[1] Prehension is said to be "feeling." Plainly the language of esthetics is the least stretched. The very word "esthetics" in English, ranging from its etymological sense of the immediately "sensory" to the acquired lofty designation for studies of the beautiful, justifies Whitehead's use. Here he does not so much stretch a term as he does accept its already broad usage. "Creativity," "feeling," "esthetic"—these are the master concepts. Religious value can hardly be fully exploited without the language of beauty. Moral value has little lure where it condemns, opposes, or ignores the sense of beauty. And social value is too expressible in humanocentric terms alone. Whitehead is concerned with the cosmic order, not just the human one. If one undertakes to use value terms other than the esthetic ones, their usefulness as general terms shows up immediately. Try explaining compassion (as opposed to justice and equality) in the language of morality, or the static splendor of a snowflake in the language of social dynamics. Better to call it "God's handiwork." At least that somewhat treacherous notion keeps the element of wonder intact.

Whitehead thus speaks of the "feeling of evil" as "aesthetic destruction" (*AI,* 330). "All order," he says, in a strong passage, "is therefore aesthetic order, and the moral order is merely certain aspects of aesthetic order" (*RM,* 105). This is the conclusion to a brief critique of Kant. Kant, says Whitehead, saw that the moral order, as a primary datum itself, made no sense without the postulation of a deity. No proof is involved in this claim of Kant's, of course, unless we choose to broaden the term "proof" to include the exhibiting of what one has to begin with, in order to follow a line of investigation. Whitehead has no quarrel with the method of demonstration. On the contrary, he wishes to extend it. Whitehead's point is that the moral necessity for a Deity is just a subdivision of the esthetic necessity for Him, the esthetic order being the dominant one. We return to Whitehead's theory of Deity below, but the present exposition is primarily secular.

We should not be surprised if evil then turns up as discord, and achieved value as harmony. Yet we can not even put simple minus and plus signs before these terms. For there is still the question, not only of timing ("birth at the wrong season"), but of time. Creativity is a principle of restlessness; and this restlessness materializes as Adventure: "always there are imperfect occasions better than occasions. . . of perfection. . . . Perfections of diverse types are among themselves discordant. . . . Thus the value of Discord is a tribute to the merits of Imperfection. . . . But even perfection will not bear the tedium of indefinite repetition" (*AI,* 330-32). There is a rhetorical swing to these generalizations. And they are pointedly illustrated by comparisons of Greek, Christian, Byzantine, and Chinese civilizations. But they have a technical basis—as they should, if Whitehead is a good metaphysician. The multiplicity of perfections, themselves possibly mutually inhibitive, is, on the one hand, founded in the creative power exemplified in the passage of time. On the other hand, we find it *mirrored* statically in the fact that the realm of eternal objects has no one vertex which includes all subordinate and less complex eternal objects as members. There are infinities of eternal objects and infinities of hierarchies of them. There is no "single, far-off, divine event toward which the whole creation moves," and there is no perfect and final order of things. In the passage of time there is a struggle for order—ever more inclusive order, as we shall see—but the indefinite number of possible types of definite perfection is the static picture of the endlessness of time. As Plato had said, "Time is the moving image of eternity." Whitehead's temporal actualizations are the moving ingressions of eternal objects.

So much for value. We must leave off reifying it, and examine it in basic form, namely as a process: valuation.

III *Valuation*

Valuation begins as self-valuation, but it extends both backward and forward in time. It extends into the immediate past, for that is what the actual occasion prehends. And if there be an enduring object of some longevity, its constituent conceptual prehensions extend "backward" much further than to the immediate past. Moreover, it extends into the indefinite future, for the completion of the act of self-valuation means the objectification of that occasion as a set of possible values for future occasions.

The sequence of the nine categories of obligation was shown to be the ordinal series of stages, by and large, in the internal development of an actual occasion. This same series can be roughly reviewed as the phases of valuation. But in the review we must pay greater attention to the elements in process which are not immediate ingredients of the actual occasion.

According to Whitehead, a valuation has three principal features: (1) It is "dependent on the other feelings in its phase of origination"; (2) it "determines in what status the eternal object has ingression into the integrated nexus physically felt", (3) it grades "the intensive importance accorded to the eternal object" as part of the whole complex of feelings (*PR*, 369). How a valuation occurs thus is a function of the totality of feelings that "enter" the occasion-in-process, the mode of the ingression, and its relative significance. Human examples are again best here. Suppose I come into my warm study. That warmth, the sight of work laid out to do, the pleasure of a coffee-feeling in the stomach, will normally integrate into a completed mild contentment having just enough edge on it, just enough "contrast" in it (contrasts, of which there are an indefinite number, constitute the eighth category of existence), so that my next acts of consciousness and their bodily counterparts will fall into a chain of steps to the desk: rereading of the present chapter, consultation of notes, reviewing of points to be made; and presently I am at work. This cozy scene, fresh from the pages of a nineteenth-century English novel, could be quite different, even with every room condition as before. Antecedent experiences, still fresh to my oncoming moment of consciousness, and therefore capable of being grasped purely conceptually without renewed physical stimulus, might have left a bad taste in my mouth or a foul odor in my nose. Or I may remember that the room has been stuffy. It's adequately warm. Never mind the warmth; let's clear out the staleness. The warmth thus functions in quite a different subjective form, although it is the same sense datum. It is discounted, we might say. In this moment of consciousness (perhaps with some purpose—some "subjective intensity"—left over which will be accessible to the next moment) I outright reject the work to be done, though the mere sensa are the same, and their *significance as to what object they stand for.* I am on my way to the window, to open it. Or again I enter the "same" room. with the same conditions. I am tired, I have a cold. The work is uninviting, the manuscript seems disorganized, the room is not warm enough. Again I ignore the writing. I get out an auxiliary heater, build up the fire in the main stove, and so on. A camera and an appropriate array of related technical equipment would have "recorded" identical scenes in these cases. But I am no camera; I enter, bearing my history, with all its polyphase elements, with me. At each point of consciousness, by the dead drift or the automated machinery called habit, by conscious reflection, by inquisitive thought, I draw together the giant history of my body and the environment it blends into, my immediate past and the fixed world it shades into; I then adjust all these prehensions to one another in this one integral practical present fact—my life through this brief patch of time. The self-integrative act is an evaluative one, for these things must be given varying weights and degrees of importance—bringing into a single synthesis a vast array of lesser evaluations, no one of which carries a fixed value rating on it. That rating it gets from *me,* within the broad range permitted by its status in the realm of eternal objects, and the antecedent functionings of my body. These are what Whitehead calls "limitations" in *Science and the Modern World.*[2] In *Process and Reality* Whitehead says, "The subject, thus constituted, is the autonomous master of its own concrescence into subject-superject. It passes from a subjective aim in concrescence into a superject with objective immortality. At any stage it is subject-superject. According to this explanation, self-determination is always imaginative in its origin" (*PR*, 374).

We pause here to underscore the ideas thus far. (1) The term "creativity" suggests, perhaps too much, the mysterious or the magical. "Autonomous master" is a good antidote. It suggests the presider over and controller of a pattern of action. (2) The term "superject" is overdue in this essay, but by now should be clear in context, and with its etymology exposed. A subject is a thing thrown under or down. Whitehead's neologism, "superject," designates the outcome, in objective immortality, of a thing thrown up, over, forward. In the passage of time it crystalizes, dropping its subjectivity, but not its existence. Past existence is a mode of existence, not the vanishing of it. (3) Finally, we turn to the coupling of self-determination and imagination. The theme is stated quickly here, to get on with the rest. Taken slow it makes a fine point. Freedom is not absence of determination, it is self-determination. Absence of determination is—at best—sheer possibility. All existence is at bottom determinate. The common tendency is to regard this as meaning that it is predetermined: only the past has original power; the present is only the automatic outcome. But which past? For any past has its past, and there is a regress of these pasts over the backward horizon of time, ad infinitum. Observational science may be able to live with this mystery by shrugging its shoulders as to the origins of causal patterns; but it cannot transfer its mode of thinking deterministically back into subjective awareness, for there we commonly recognize the difference between *compelled reactions* like those of pain, for example, and sensation, and *imaginative generations* which identify ourselves for ourselves as agents. Imagination is required in the solving of problems, the creation of an object or an idea, and so on. In the latter cases we know ourselves as the origin of the compulsion, not merely as its target. Imagination and self-determination are complementary notions.

IV *God*

This is as far as we can go without introducing the idea of God. The general subject of valuation and the just-mentioned one of agency both lead inevitably to this idea. Whitehead says, "The primordial created fact is the unconditioned conceptual valuation of the entire multiplicity of eternal objects. This is the 'primordial nature' of God" (*PR,* 46). Whitehead shortly continues, "Apart from God, eternal objects unrealized in the actual world would be relatively non-existent for the concrescence in question. For effective relevance requires agency of comparison, and agency belongs exclusively to actual occasions" *(ibid.).*

The central idea here is God's role as embracing—in "conceptual valuation"—the "multiplicity" of eternal objects, those possible values which are concretely actualized in the passage of nature. But we need to lay our ground with some care, for this primordial nature of God is but one aspect of Him. To begin with, what necessity is there for introducing deity at all?

1. *Historical conceptions of God.* In sweeping but suggestive caricature Whitehead traces the origins of three main ideas of God: (a) the "Eastern Asiatic" one of an impersonal order, immanent in the world; (b) the "Semitic" one of a personal creator, upon whom the existence of the world depends, therefore a transcendent God; and (c) the "Pantheistic" one that, monistically, identifies God and Reality (*RM,* 68-69). Spinoza's view is the best example of the last. Efforts to bring these separate insights into mutual support will, as Whitehead says, "lead to complexity of thought" (*RM,* 70). Each of these three notions plays some part in Whitehead's own conception of deity, the third sharply modified. The principal sources of the Christian idea of God are somewhat less diversified. They stem from the Semitic conception of a personal God endowed "with the rationality of a Greek philosopher" (*SMW,* 18). This essentially medieval conception, embodied in medieval theology, Whitehead regards as underlying the *impetus* of modern science. Whitehead says that "faith in the possibility of science," before the emergence of any genuine modern scientific theory is "an unconscious derivative from medieval theology" (*SMW,* 19; cf. *RM,* 33). This theme is always in the background of his thought and emerges articulately from time to time. Elsewhere, he speaks of the notion of a rational providence as leading, for example, to "the trust in the order of nature" (*SMW,* 90). The previous passage goes on to explain that science develops an active interest in the ordinary course of affairs "for their own sake."

It is important not to misunderstand this claim. Whitehead says *unconscious.* He does not suppose that men defended faith in God or faith in the order of nature, by reference of the one to the other. He is referring to a wholeness of conviction about the order of things, which was secularizable. This secularization—as in the case of Newton, for instance—represented no challenge to religious devotion. It was merely pursuable without constant reference to theology. Historically, the idea of a stable providence provides the matrix from which one draws his conception of a stable order of nature. To be sure, Hume had held that his faith was founded on its practicality alone—we have nothing else to go on, in our conduct of practical affairs. If one puts Whitehead in dialectical confrontation with old-fashioned, primitive atheism of the 1920's and 1930's (the time in which he was writing), it would come out like this: "Very well, doubt Deity—but then share Hume's modesty and his caution. The same reasons that lead Hume to espouse practicality, rather than God, as the foundation of our sense of order in nature, lead him also to reject all over-arching principles, including the demonstrability of causal structures of the world, the quantitative approach to reality, and so on. If you are going to be cautious about how far you go with your faith, be consistent. Don't reject the overwhelming intuitions—vague, conflicting, and difficult to clarify—that the race has had of divinity, withdrawing the investment of faith in these intuitions, only to reinvest it in Clocks and Rods Incorporated. If religion gives no certain account of the whole order of the world, neither does observational science."

Plainly, for Whitehead the order of nature is a problem for both science and religion. Nor is he willing to accept the natural superiority of the one over the other. It is typical that in a work called *Science and the Modern World* he should trace the origins of science to its religious springs; however, in *Religion in the Making* he says, "reason is the safeguard of the objectivity of religion: it secures for it the general coherence denied to hysteria" (*RM*, 64). Moreover, "Religious truth must be developed from knowledge acquired when our ordinary senses and intellectual operations are at their highest pitch of discipline" (*RM*, 123). More compactly, in *Science and the Modern World* in the chapter on Religion and Science, he says in the same vein: "Religion will not regain its old power until it can face change in the same spirit as does science" (*SMW*, 270).

2. *The Order of Nature.* The restriction on science is thus not that it

opposes the dogmas of religion. These need constant criticism and revision (*RM*, Chapter 4). It is that it deals with the abstractly factual side of existence. There is thus a massive case of the "Fallacy of Misplaced Concreteness" if science be raised to cosmology. "The peculiar character of religious truth is that it explicitly deals with values. It brings into our consciousness that permanent side of the universe which we can care for. It thereby provides a meaning, in terms of value, for our own existence, a meaning which flows from the nature of things" (*RM*, 124)

Whitehead's argument from here on out is not to be confused with logical proof, nor with systematic organization of fact. These domains, with which he was well acquainted, have little to offer the problem in hand. That problem is "that there is a process of actual occasions, and the fact that the occasions are the emergence of values. . . ." But "there cannot be value without antecedent standards of value" (*SMW*, 256). An actuality is a value for itself, but from a past of variegated values and for a future which will value it in different ways. Whitehead's argument seems to be that if all actuality is interconnected and each least unit has only a brief space, the more prevailing order must be referred to something other than the present moment of becoming. The development of the idea of God arises as an explanation of intuitions deeply felt rather than as a doctrinal artillery shell trained on the target of unbelief. The intuitions are basically two. We have just had brief looks at both of them: (1) that the becoming of value is transient, but (2) that value becomes by reference to something behind it, something more permanent that we "care for." What is required, Whitehead says, is a "principle of limitation." God himself has a limitation; it is false that he is "in all respects infinite." This limitation is his goodness (*RM*, 153). Of the conventional omniscience, omnibenevolence, and omnipotence, Whitehead eliminates the last, on familiar grounds: if God is omnipotent He is the source of evil, as well as of good. What is it, then, that we worship? His goodness.

But the elimination of the problem of evil in itself supplies little positive doctrine, let alone persuasion. Whitehead denies the attribute of omnipotence to God because it runs counter to the deep urging toward permanence of value which we feel, and which each actual occasion embodies in some way, however small. "There is an actual world because there is an order in nature" (*RM*, 104). And, "There is nothing actual which could be actual without some measure of order" (*RM*, 119). The order requires reference, moreover, to value, since we are dealing with what is concrete. God is not all-powerful. His role as a limitation on the course of nature is one with the fact that He has a limitation: His goodness. How is this role exercised?

3. *God's Function.* God's purpose is the attainment of value, and this is a creative purpose (*RM*, 104; cf. 100). But the question as to God's role or His purpose is faintly ambiguous. It can be answered either by asking what is God's status in the world or in a systematic description of it. These two themes should hardly be divorced. However, we have been dealing with an exposition of Whitehead's systematic thought. Accordingly, we look at the systematic status of God first.

(a) In *Religion in the Making* Whitehead discerns three "formative elements" in the temporal world—creativity, eternal objects, and the actual, nontemporal entity, God. The description of God given in this list is compact and later explicated: He is that entity "whereby the indetermination of mere creativity is transmuted into a determinate freedom" (*RM*, 90). He is thus "The Principle of Concretion" (*SMW*, 250). Without God the other two formative elements would "fail in their functions" (*RM*, 104). The creativity presents us with "infinite freedom." And the eternal objects (the "realm of forms") gives us infinite possibilities, but neither is adequate by itself to explain the actual. Why so? Because whatever is actualized is thereby finite, limited, representing just *this* order of value and none other.

These themes from *Religion in the Making* shed light upon the all-too-compact Chapter XI of *Science and the Modern World*, where Whitehead says that "every actual occasion is a limitation imposed on possibility" (*SMW*, 251). Further, he states that "Restriction is the price of [concrete] value," and that "God is the ultimate limitation, and His existence is the ultimate irrationality" (*SMW*, 256, 257). This ultimate irrationality is no reappearance of antirationalism as a defense of religion. We recall that, according to *Process and Reality,* actual entities are the only "reasons," and that there is no "going behind them." The giant fact of nature, in Whitehead's view, is that there is an order of nature which is the embodiment of values. This does not mean that there is no real evil, no antivalues in the course of nature. "There is evil when things are at cross-purposes" (*RM*, 97). And God is to be understood in this respect as being only the "completed ideal harmony" (*RM*, 120). One gets the sense that God's task is as endless as time itself. But as a fact—*the* fact, indeed—the order of nature also requires explanation. And if we say "Why is there an order of nature?" the answer must be given in terms of an actual entity. Such an actual entity would be a rock-bottom explanation, behind which one cannot go, and in this sense is "irrational," not as an exception to reason but "the ground of rationality" (*SMW*, 257), that is of a rational order of nature. This is not the doctrine, "I believe because it is absurd," but rather, "I believe because it is absurd not to believe."

(b) Thus the account of the systematic status of God has introduced the more primary theme of God's role in the world as partially portrayed by the systematic position discerned for Him. Systematically He stands as an abiding agent. This is what is meant by saying He is a nontemporal entity. It does not mean that temporality and God are divorced from one another. Quite the contrary: it means that God is an entity not given to temporal completeness and perishing, like all other actual entities—those called "occasions." He is "never in the past. . . ." (*PR*, 47). He is everlasting.[3] His abiding role as an abiding agent is that of conjoiner of unlimited possibility with unlimited creativity in the production of finite actual occasions embodying a concrete order of value. By now it is evident that God's role as the "principle of concretion" is complex. Two questions must be raised. (1) Are all the agency functions of this God arrangeable under one nature? Whitehead's ultimate answer to this is a candid "No." (2) What about the object of *worship,* where persistence in many forms throughout history, constitutes one of the main reasons for our having to turn our attention to God in the first place? And what of this enshrined impersonal "Principle"? Does God's role in Whitehead's system of thought warrant Him as an object of worship in the traditional Western sense? The answer here partly depends on the answer to the earlier question. For the moment it must be an unsatisfactory "Yes and No."

4. *The Two Natures of God.* The foregoing analysis has largely been in terms of *Science and the Modern World* and *Religion in the Making,* in the interests of introductory clarification. The most detailed treatment of the ideas of God is in *Religion in the Making.* But the

maturity of Whitehead's exposition appears in *Process and Reality*. It is in this work that he brings out the duality which we have seen partially submerged in his prior exposition. The duality arises because the function of "concretion" has two aspects.

(a) *The Primordial nature of God.* We have now returned to our starting point of the subject of "God" in His primordial nature. This is His "conceptual side." An actual occasion has a mental pole whose function is to grasp eternal objects. Whitehead speaks of this grasp as "conceptual." The actual nontemporal entity similarly holds "the entire multiplicity" of eternal objects in His conceptual grasp. We may be reminded of "God, for whom all things are possible," but the meaning is different here. It might be better to say, "God, for whom all possibles are things." This conceptual grasp is to be taken with a word of caution. It is "pure," utterly devoid of physical reference (*PR*, 48-49), and therefore nonconscious. Consciousness, we recall, requires "impure" prehensions rooted in both physical and conceptual prehensions. Not only is God, as primordial, not conscious (see also *PR*, 522), He is "unbounded by contradiction" (*PR*, 528). This violation of our devotion to logic is also not an invitation to the riot of absurdity which often passes for religious insight. The lack of contradiction is merely a function of the lack of actuality. If God's primordial nature includes the whole realm of eternal objects, as mere possibles, it necessarily holds contraries and outright contradictions equally. Every actualization, we recall, is a *decision,* a cutting-off, a choosing of this and *not that.* There is nothing exotic about the entertainment, conceptually, of contradictions. Any man in the severity of a need for choice knows that a decision is preceded commonly by the prior envisagement of gross incompatibles. God as primordial is not only deficient in actuality, unbounded by considerations of contradiction, but further, eternal—like the eternal objects—and limited by no actuality (*PR*, 524). As presenting—so to speak—all possibilities, God is not emotionally blank, "He is the lure for feeling [this was also said of propositions, we recall], the eternal urge of desire" (*PR*, 522). Whitehead goes on to compare Aristotle's "Unmoved Mover" to this notion, but reminds us that, since conceptual prehension is necessarily evaluative in form, we cannot think of the Primordial Nature satisfactorily merely as an object of thought.

If we now ask to what extent is this (metaphysical) nature of God a suitable object of worship, the answer is not clean-cut. An emporium of possible values can hardly be said itself to be value-indifferent. Whitehead's "Primordial Nature of God" is somewhat warmer than Aristotle's "Prime Mover," whose status as a lure for thought rather smothers its role as a lure for feeling. But there is a deficiency of actuality, and "It is deflected neither by love, nor by hatred, for what in fact comes to pass" (*PR*, 522).

There is a striving in all things, says Spinoza. Whitehead agrees, with some qualifications. This striving is toward the realization of some value. However universal this urge, it is the creature who lays his own definiteness on the achievement of value. In fact that definiteness of value and the creature's are one. The sheer universality of the urge, posing before us all possibility, oblivious to fact, logic, love, or hate, thus really has only the *emotive* tone necessary for *objects* of worship. Perhaps the Greek mind, not so preoccupied—or obsessed—with our kind of individualism, could award a position of respect or even a kind of intellectual reverence to such an entity. That element of respect, which dominates Greek thinking from Achilles to Plato's *The Good* and Aristotle's *Prime Mover,* is not enough. It passes by the sense of acute subjective personality and love which arises in the Semitic strain of our religious thinking.

(b) *The Consequent Nature of God.* This latter conception, cast to be sure in metaphysical language and reflection, and largely voided of earlier and cruder anthropomorphism, comes out in the Consequent Nature of God. This nature is "derivative" and arises from the "creative advance of the world" (*PR*, 523-24). This is the nature of God of which Whitehead says that it is "never in the past." This is God's status as both "determined" and "incomplete," as well as 'everlasting,' fully actual, and conscious" (*PR*, 524). We see that the nontemporality spoken of in *Religion in the Making* has surfaced here in two forms to match the two natures. The nontemporality of the primordial nature is its eternity, its unalterability, and its inaccessibility to any passage of fact. The nontemporality of the consequent nature is in its abidingness, its everlastingness, its incompleteness, its constant totalization without the issuing of a final totality. And this unendingness is the principal qualification—mentioned above, on Whitehead's employment of the Pantheistic as well as the impersonal and personal traditions. It also represents, at the very least, a strong deviation from much of conventional Christian theology.

If we now return to our question about objects of worship, it is clear that the Consequent Nature of God embodies most of what is needed. Our clearest intuition of the Primordial Nature is through the primitive urge toward some value. This urge is exemplified in all life—if it be only toward the value of sheer survival. But this Primordial Nature is deficient in one critical respect. It invokes no faith, no hope, no charity—or love (*caritas*). Love as eros, perhaps, but as *caritas,* no. To be sure, there have been powerful religions in which these spiritual attitudes play but little part. It is difficult to say what are the indispensable features of all worship—apart from awe and wonder. Whitehead gives a half-dozen or so definitions of religion, in *Religion in the Making,* each from a particular angle, or in some context. Perhaps the most penetrating, for modern purposes, is, "Religion is what the individual does with his own solitariness" (*RM,* 16). But deeper than this runs the still less theistic, "Religion is force of belief cleansing the inward parts" (*RM,* 15). It seems clear, both from Whitehead's religious background, and from the tone of his philosophical thought, that he is undertaking to give a common basis for the highest vision in religious belief. He can hardly eschew the distinctive achievements in Christian religious thought. Thus, any general definition of religion, wide enough to cover all religions, must avoid theistic reference. But Whitehead's own *convictions* introduce the nature of God.

(c) *The Transcendence of Evil.* The dominant term in Whitehead's explication is "tender" (repeatedly, *PR,* 525-26). Tenderness suggests the abundant concern that faith believes in, hope waits for, and charity embodies. And this is enough to show to which side of God's duality, worship is addressed. The word "tender," however, should not be divorced from its less emotional moorings as well. Who "tends," conserves. And this is the principal role of Whitehead's Consequent Nature of God. We have seen that the evil of the world arises "when things are at cross purposes." This is the evil in which the world loses by conflict of aim, but "The ultimate evil in the temporal world is deeper than any specific evil. It lies in the fact that the past fades, that time is a 'perpetual perishing' " (*PR,* 517). Victor and vanquished and the quarrel between them are washed away. Yes, but only from the point of view of what they accomplish in their own completed (and compromised) subjective aims. "The completion of God's nature into a fulness of physical feeling is derived from the objectification of the world in God. . . . his derivative nature is consequent upon the creative advance of the world" (*PR*, 523-24). And is insofar as incomplete as the world itself. (*PR*, 529). The tenderness is that "nothing be lost . . . nothing . . . can be saved. . . . He does not create the world, he saves it" (*PR'* 525-26).

Objective immortality of actual occasions is the death of their subjective aims. But these occasions are "externally free." They are definite, "determinate" as to actualization. They can still serve the future in innumerable ways. Other actual occasions to come will use them diversely. The category of relativity (No. iv of Explanation, *PR*, 33) states "That the potentiality for being an element in a real concrescence of many entities into one actuality, is the *one general metaphysical character attaching to all entities*, actual and non-actual" (italics mine). God is no exception. His concrescence is continuous. His aim, like that of all actual entities, is at a unity. This process of unification is terminal for actual occasions, but everlasting for the "non-temporal" entity. The goodness of God is actualized not only in His saving and holding in His nature what otherwise is carried into the mere past; but also bringing into unity what was before in conflict: "God's purpose in the creative advance is the evocation of intensities" (*PR*, 161); "What is inexorable in God, is valuation as an aim towards 'order'; and "order" means "society" permissive of actualities with patterned intensity of feeling arising from *adjusted* contrasts" (*PR*, 373-374; italics mine).

Whitehead was reared in a Christian household. Christianity holds that faith requires a perspective beyond the narrow conceits of selfhood. Whitehead's last words in *Process and Reality* are,

God is the great companion—the fellow-sufferer who understands.

We find here the final application of the doctrine of objective immortality. Throughout the perishing occasions in the life of each temporal Creature, the inward source of distaste or of refreshment, the judge arising out of the very nature of things, redeemer or goddess of mischief, is the transformation of Itself, everlasting in the Being of God.

In this way, the insistent craving is justified—the insistent craving that zest for existence be refreshed by the ever-present, unfading importance of our immediate actions, which perish and yet live for evermore. (*PR*, 532-33)

Notes and References

Chapter One

1. The biographical materials used here come principally from three sources: (1) those listed under the category of "personal" in *Essays in Science and Philosophy* (New York: Philosophical Library, 1947); (2) William Ernest Hocking's essay, "Whitehead as I knew Him," in *Alfred North Whitehead: Essays on His Philosophy*, ed. by George Kline (Englewood Cliffs: Prentice-Hall, 1963), reprinted from *The Journal of Philosophy*, 58:505-16, 1961), and (3) conversations with Mrs. Whitehead in the spring of 1958. There is a present biography being written by Professor Victor Lowe, which will clarify and correct this and many other biographical sketches.

2. See Nathaniel Lawrence, *Whitehead's Philosophical Development* (Berkeley: University of California Press, 1956). The minimizing of this aspect of Whitehead's philosophical thought robs an astonishingly creative mind of its power for rethinking and thinking anew.

3. I remember the same sense of style and personal dignity in a visiting Tory lady whose financial and social station were ones of great modesty. I said to her, when her political persuasions became evident, that it must have been quite a shock when Lord Bertrand Russell renounced his title. "Oh no," she said, "We were veddy glad."

4. Hocking in Kline, p. 13.

5. *Ibid.*

6. Victor Lowe, quoting from Russell: "Whatever historical subjects came up he could always supply some illuminating fact. . . ." *Understanding Whitehead* (Baltimore: Johns Hopkins Press, 1962), p. 8.

7. The larger part of what follows here is taken from Hocking's "Whitehead as I knew Him."

8. Lawrence Henderson, biologist and author of *The Fitness of the Environment* and other works; Henry Osborn Taylor, historian and author of *The Medieval Mind* and other works.

9. Unknown to Whitehead, of course.

Chapter Two

1. This constitutes one of the arguments, for example, for a certain kind of immortality in the *Phaedo,* which see. The psyche is there treated as the direct opposite of death. The psyche is thus the absence of death, not its victim.

179

2. See Section 8, God, this chapter, and Chapter 9.

3. By an unreduced vocabulary I mean the use of "organism," for instance, to designate what is not reducible to explanation as a "mechanism" or the use of "feeling" to designate something more than what can be translated into physico-chemical response.

4. See especially Chapter 2, "Theories of the Bifurcation of Nature."

5. See William James, "Does Consciousness Exist?" in *Essays in Radical Empiricism* reprinted with *Pluralistic Universe.* (New York: Longmans Green, 1958). pp. 1-38.

6. Chapters 5-7.

7. See *SMW,* Chapters 5 and 6.

8. One may guess that any exposition of Whitehead's philosophy by himself or others will require recurrence to the same themes again and again, each time from a different angle and in a different context. The reader should examine Whitehead's own statement of this notion on p. vii of *PR.* The point is that one reads, writes, and tends to think linearly, one thing after another. Yet speculative philosophy, like any vision, tends to grasp things in a *Gestalt,* wholly. There is bound to be a weakness in sheer serial exposition of a multidimensional view of the world. This weakness can be partly overcome by returning to basic notions and using them as points of new departure along (monodimensional) lines exposing systems of relation not before noticed. As Whitehead indicates, this is his method, one which requires the redundancy of topic that has irritated and alienated some otherwise thoughtful readers. My own conviction is that this weblike character of reality creeps into individual sentences in Whitehead's more difficult works, e.g., *PR.* For this reason, he is sometimes condemned as unintelligible, even by critics acquainted with polyadic logics. The point is too technical to be pursued here further, but in general I would say that some of the knottier problems in Whitehead can best be unraveled—conceivably *only* unraveled—by attending to a weblike syntax in his exposition, admittedly a strain upon our conventional conceptions of syntax and logic.

9. See the *Confessions,* Book XI.

10. *Philosophy of Mathematics and Natural Science* (New York: Atheneum, 1963), p. 116.

11. Also as sounds and scents; see *SMW,* p. 151.

12. Readers familiar with Kierkegaard may remark that Judge Wilhelm in *Either/Or* insists that who chooses the ethical chooses not the good over the evil but good *and* evil.

Chapter Three

1. What follows here is a simplification of *PR,* pp. 317-72. The themes are subtle and complex, occasionally obscure. They raise

problems for study in depth, but these problems require a technical realm, which can only be partially invaded in the later chapters of this book.

2. The passages referred to here are in a section of *PR* which has been largely lifted, with little change, frcm an earlier work, *Symbolism, Its Meaning and Effect*, largely pp. 255-79.

Chapter Four

1. See Lawrence, pp. 291-99, for a more detailed treatment.
2. On the Fallacy of Misplaced Concreteness see Lawrence, pp. 322-25.
3. The initial draft of this book was written during the period in which cardiologists all over the world were waiting to see if a transplanted heart in a South African would continue to be accepted by its new body.

Chapter Five

1. See the Category of Explanation, Number 11, *PR*, p. 35.
2. Whitehead's first generalizations of the subject are contained in *The Principle of Relativity*, a book showing how the theory of perception must be framed to provide a context for the relativity theory of measurement, and providing a treatment of the scientific theory designed to solve certain philosophical problems in the customary presentation.

Chapter Six

1. See Lawrence, Chapter 22.
2. The present author doesn't think that this is so. For example, what about wet rain making the ground wet? Aren't there abundant examples of transfer from cause to effect where there is continuity of quality? This example hardly closes debate, to be sure, and is assailable, but it seems to be a line of thought not investigated by Hume. In any case, our interest here is in Hume's views as seen by Whitehead.
3. There are references to Hume in the index of *Process and Reality* covering over 100 pages of its 533 pages of text—just about a fifth of the book.
4. New York: Scribner's, 1923, especially pp. 17ff.
5. See Maurice Merleau-Ponty, *The Structure of Behavior* (Boston: Beacon Press, 1963). Merleau-Ponty is clearly running on a track close to Whitehead when he says, "There is an exchange of service between the description of the phenomenal body and causal explanation" (p.

157). This remark is made in the context of a discussion of perception and its physico-chemical basis. Merleau-Ponty gives us related comment, in a footnote to Buytendyk (Chapter 3, note 68, pp. 243-44) and then (p. 159) quotes a surprisingly Whiteheadian passage from the biologist Uexkull, who differs only from Whitehead in his more poetic statement: "Every organism is a melody which sings itself." See also, Merleau-Ponty, *The Phenomenology of Perception,* Part I, and J.-P. Sartre, *Being and Nothingness,* Pt. III, Chapter 2.

Chapter Eight

1. See Lawrence, Chapter 6.
2. "Immortality," in P.A. Schilpp, ed. *The Philosophy of Alfred North Whitehead* (New York: Tudor, 2nd ed. 1951), p. 692.
3. There is another classification of the modes of ingression into four at *PR,* p. 249. This is somewhat clumsily wrought. The distinctions are reducible to the three just given from p. 445. They have the advantage, however, of introducing the important notions of "conformal feelings" and "comparative feelings."

Chapter Nine

1. See Nathaniel Lawrence, "The Vision of Beauty and the Temporality of Deity in Whitehead's Philosophy," in Kline, pp. 168-78, for further elaboration of this point and related themes.
2. See Lawrence, pp. 273-279 for a somewhat more detailed analysis.
3. See Lawrence, "Vision of Beauty," pp. 172-74.

Bibliography

A list of Whitehead's works cited or used in this essay. (Abbreviations used in citation follow the titles.)

A Treatise on Universal Algebra, with Applications. Cambridge: Cambridge University Press, 1898.

An Introduction to Mathematics. New York: Henry Holt, 1911. (Home University Library.)

An Enquiry Concerning the Principles of Natural Knowledge. Cambridge: Cambridge University Press, 1919; second edition, 1925. *(PNK)*

The Concept of Nature. *Cambridge: Cambridge University Press, 1920. (CN)*

The Principle of Relativity, with Applications to Physical Science. Cambridge: Cambridge University Press, 1922. *(Rel)*

Science and the Modern World. New York: Macmillan, 1925. *(SMW)*

Religion in the Making. New York: Macmillan, 1926. *(RM)*

Symbolism, Its Meaning and Effect. New York: Macmillan, 1927. *(Sym)*

The Aims of Education and Other Essays. New York: Macmillan, 1929. *(AE)*

The Function of Reason. Princeton: Princeton University Press, 1929. *(FR)*

Process and Reality. New York: Macmillan, 1929. *(PR)*

Adventures of Ideas. New York: Macmillan, 1933. *(AI)*

Modes of Thought. New York, Macmillan, 1938. *(MT)*

Essays in Science and Philosophy. New York: Philosophical Library, 1947.

(With Bertrand Russell) *Principia Mathematica.* 3 volumes. Cambridge: Cambridge University Press, 1910-13.

Recommended commentators.

CHRISTIAN, WILLIAM A. *An Interpretation of Whitehead's Metaphysics.* New Haven: Yale University Press, 1959.

KLINE, GEORGE L. (ed.). *Alfred North Whitehead: Essays on His Philosophy.* Englewood Cliffs, N.J.: Prentice-Hall, 1963.

LAWRENCE, NATHANIEL. *Whitehead's Philosophical Development: A Critical History of the Background of Process and Reality.* Berkeley: University of California Press, 1956.

LECLERC, IVOR. *Whitehead's Metaphysics: An Introductory Exposition.* New York: Macmillan, 1958.

LOWE, VICTOR. *Understanding Whitehead.* Baltimore: Johns Hopkins Press, 1962.

PALTER, ROBERT M. *Whitehead's Philosophy of Science.* Chicago: University of Chicago Press, 1960.

SCHILPP, P. A. (ed.). *The Philosophy of Alfred North Whitehead.* 2nd edition. New York: Tudor, 1951. (Library of Living Philosophers, Vol. 3.)

SHERBURNE, DONALD W. *A Whiteheadian Aesthetic: Some Implications of Whitehead's Metaphysical Speculation.* New Haven: Yale University Press, 1961.

Index

Abstraction, 146-47; extensive, method of, 149
Actual entity. *See* Entity, actual
Actual occasion. *See* Occasion, actual
Aim, subjective, 129, 176
Appearance, defined, 110
Aristotle, 30, 35, 53, 54, 65, 79, 98, 137, 139; prime mover of, 53-54, 65, 173, 174
Augustine, Saint, 50

Becoming, 69-70
Berkeley, George, 38, 90
Bifurcation of nature. *See* Nature, bifurcation of
Biography of an actual occasion. See Occasion, actual, biography of an
Body. *See* Physicality for main entry; lived, 136; withness of the, 128; and mind, 90-119.
   See also Mind-body problem
Broad, C.D. 99

Canalization, 44
Causa sui. See Cause of itself
Causal efficacy. *See* Efficacy, causal
Causality (causation, cause), 59, 112, 117, 118, 155. *See also* Efficacy, causal
Causation, efficient, 36, 37, 44, 53, 55, 70, 80, 155; final 36, 55; self, *See* Cause of itself; teleological, *See* Telos
Cause, past as, 52-53; of itself, 37, 63, 110
Coherence, 49-51, 157
Comparative feeling. *See* Feeling, comparative
Conceptual prehension. *See* Prehension, conceptual; revision, *see* Revision, conceptual; valuation, *see* Valuation, conceptual
Concrescence, 72-73
Concreteness, misplaced, 87, 97, 109-11, 146; fallacy, of, 87, 110, 170
Concretion, principle of, 171, 172
Conformity, temporal, 135-36
Connection, extensive, 23, 121, 149, 155; method of, 23, 121, 149
Conscious perception. *See* Perception, conscious
Consciousness, 40, 42, 47, 72, 75, 89, 93, 95, 100, 108, 113-14, 120-41, 173; human, 76; stream of, 40; of value, 48-49